WALKING THE
RIVER RHINE TRAIL
GERMANY

Burg Rheinfels, St Goar (Stage 8)

WALKING THE RIVER RHINE TRAIL GERMANY

by
Alan Castle

CICERONE PRESS
MILNTHORPE, CUMBRIA, UK

© A. Castle 1999
ISBN 185284 276 8
A catalogue record for this book is available from the British Library.

> *Wealth I ask not, hope nor love,*
> *Nor a friend to know me;*
> *All I seek, the heaven above,*
> *And the road below me.*

Songs of Travel - The Vagabond
R.L. Stevenson

To Ted & P.P.

Photographs and illustrations by the author

ACKNOWLEDGEMENTS

I am indebted, as always, to my wife, Beryl Castle, for all her advice, support and encouragement during the planning and writing of this guidebook. Thanks also go to Waltraud Bündgen of the Fremdenverkehrs und Heilbäderverband, Rheinland-Pfalz, for information on the many attractions and tourist facilities of the Rhine Valley.

Other guidebooks by Alan Castle for Cicerone:
Tour of the Queyras (French & Italian Alps) - 1990.
The Robert Louis Stevenson Trail (Cévennes, France) - 1992.
Walks In Volcano Country (Auvergne and Velay, France) - 1992.
Walking the French Gorges (Provence and the Ardèche) - 1993.
The Brittany Coastal Path - 1995.
Walking in the Ardennes - 1996.
A Pyrenean Trail (GR 10) - New Edition 1997.

Front cover: A view of Gründelbachtal from Burg Rheinfels - the Rhein-höhenweg passes through this attractive valley (Stage 8)

CONTENTS

Advice to Readers

Readers are advised that whilst every effort is taken by the author to ensure the accuracy of this guidebook, changes can occur which may affect the contents. It is advisable to check locally on transport, accommodation, opening hours, shops etc but even rights-of-way can be altered.

The publisher would welcome notes of any such changes

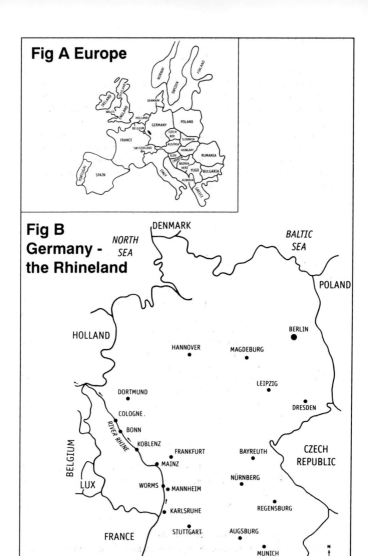

Fig A Europe

Fig B Germany - the Rhineland

Introduction

WALKING IN GERMANY
There are several hundred thousand kilometres of waymarked walking trails in Germany, the majority of which are adequately waymarked and well maintained. A great many are local routes, sometimes linear but very often circular in nature (*Rundwanderwege*), of varying length but typically from 8 to 40km, ideal for either a few hours' easy strolling, or a long, relatively hard day on the hills and through the forests. The circular routes often start and end at special countryside car parks (*Wanderparkplatz*) specifically designed with countryside walkers in mind. Some of the trails originated as routes used on special *Wandertage*, after which they became established as permanent trails, available for all to walk at any time of the year. Many others are established, waymarked and maintained by local walking clubs or organisations, often sponsored by tourist offices or even private companies.

The country has an extensive network of long distance paths, passing through all the major walking areas of the country. Many of these paths, or National Trails, have distinctive waymarking symbols, by which they are recognised. This guidebook describes just one of Germany's National Walking Trails, the Rheinhöhenweg, which follows the course of the Rhine from Bonn in the north to Alsheim in the south, a distance of 273km (169.5 miles).

In addition to these National Trails the country has nine of the eleven European Long Distance Paths, or "E Routes", passing through it (the E 1, E 3, E 4, E 5, E 6, E 8, E 9, E 10 and E 11) which make up tens of thousands of kilometres of trail. (Compare this with the relatively short section of E 8 across northern England, Britain's only "E" route. See "European Long Distance Trails - The E 8 and The E 3" below.) Germany was at the forefront of the foundation of the European Rambling Association (ERA) whose remit is to establish and popularise European Long Distance Trails, and has always taken a key, active role in its organisation. (The headquarters of the ERA are in Saarbrücken, Germany - see Appendix D for their address.)

Apart from the Bavarian Alps in the south of the country, where some routes are extremely steep and exposed, the majority of the walking trails in Germany offer relatively easy grade walking. The country has quite extensive areas of woodland: a far higher percentage of the land being forested than in Britain.

Walking holidays are popular with Germans and consequently there is plenty of accommodation particularly suitable for walkers in most of the main walking areas. Apart from the ubiquitous pension, *gasthaus* and hotel, there is an extensive network of alpine huts, maintained by the German Alpine Club, in Bavaria and over the border into Austria, whilst in other areas there are many Youth Hostels as well as other forms of budget accommodation, often established and run by walking organisations, to accommodate individuals, groups and walking club meets. Above all walking in Germany is a social activity, and Germans are particularly friendly to the stranger when out walking. You will always receive a *Guten Tag*, *Morgen* or *Grüss Gott* greeting when passing other people out walking.

THE RIVER RHINE AND RHINELAND

The River Rhine (*Rhein* in German) is a major European river. 1320km (820 miles) in length, it rises in the mountains of Switzerland, forming the border between that country and first Liechtenstein, then Austria and finally Germany. From Basle it forms the German-French border for a while before entering Germany. During its crossing of this country its major tributaries are the Neckar, Main, Mosel and Ruhr, after which it enters the Netherlands, where it is known in Dutch as the Rijn. Once over the Dutch border it splits into a number of branches which link, divide and link again, forming a huge delta over the south-west corner of Holland, its waters entering the North Sea by a number of estuaries.

The River Rhine has proved throughout history to be an effective barrier to the progress of invading armies, from the Roman legions, to the Americans at Remagen in the Second World War.

A major commercial waterway, the river has through the ages helped to establish the prosperity of Europe, and today still sees a vast quantity of barge traffic. It is navigable up to Basle. In centuries past the waters of the Rhine were treacherous in many areas, and there were numerous tragic tales of craft and crew lost as a result. Nowadays the river has been controlled by a number of modern engineering techniques. Alongside the commercial traffic the river today sees many pleasure craft, particularly the Rhine Cruise Boats which carry large numbers of tourists every year between Bonn and Mainz. Within this section is the scenically spectacular Rhine Gorge, between Bingen and Koblenz, where the river narrows to twist and turn beneath precipitous rocky crags topped with scores of romantic medieval castles. All this area is covered by the River Rhine Walking

Trail.

The best known area of the River Rhine, is the section in Germany between Cologne and Worms, the river and surrounding countryside being known generally as the Rhineland. Here is a country not only of great historical importance in the development of the German nation and in the shaping of Europe itself, but also a land steeped in romantic myths and legends, the subject of epic poems, songs and paintings. Numerous picturesque medieval villages of half-timbered houses and cobbled streets dot the landscape, many of them gracing the banks of the river itself. The region also contains several of Germany's most well known and elegant cities including Cologne, Bonn, Koblenz, Wiesbaden, Mainz and Worms which, apart from being packed with history, contain some of the finest buildings, museums, cathedrals and churches in the country.

The region of the Rhine Gorge, where the river narrows, was the province of immensely rich and powerful robber barons in medieval times, who controlled the area from their mighty imposing fortresses, towering above the waters of the Rhine, demanding heavy taxes from the passing shipping. Their castles, many of them now romantic ruins, are prominent features of the region today and obvious targets for the present day tourist industry. Rhineland has always been an area that has played a significant role in the history of the German people; many memories of this will be seen along the route of the Rheinhöhenweg with, for example, monuments to Bismark, Kaiser Wilhelm, Schiller, Richard Wagner and other important figures in the history and culture of the nation.

But apart from the historical significance of the region, Rhineland is very much associated with numerous myths and legends, the major of which is undoubtedly the epic *Nibelungenlied*, the great national saga which was written at the end of the twelfth century by an unknown author. It is an extraordinary tale of heroism, treachery, vengeance and incest, of immense importance to the German inheritance. Richard Wagner's great nineteenth-century music drama *The Ring Cycle (Das Ring des Nibelungen)* was based on the Norse versions of these same legends. Here in the Rhineland is the very setting of the drama, for it was beneath the waters of this great river that the Rhine Maidens safeguarded the gold, the *Rheingold*, that is the very cornerstone of the legend.

The other great legend associated with the River Rhine is that of the Lorelei. Associated with the myth of the mermaid, the legend is that of a beautiful maiden sitting on a rock, combing the long tresses of her hair, mesmerising passing sailors and thereby luring them to a watery grave amidst the fathomless depths of the dark waters below. But there are many other less well known myths and tales associated with this region, every mile of the river between Koblenz and Mainz being crammed with history and folklore.

The spectacular natural beauty of the Rhineland is not confined to the Rhine valley itself. Several of the Rhine's tributaries form equally impressive, if less well known, valley systems, such as those of the Nahe, Lahn and Ahr, which slice though the Hunsrück, Eifel and Westerwald hill ranges which border the Rhine. The Mosel valley, which meets that of the Rhine at Koblenz, is the most famous of the Rhine tributaries, the Roman city of Trier being the best known and attractive of its many towns. Both the Rhine and the Mosel valleys are world famous for their extensive vineyards, Rhineland being the major wine producing area of Germany.

The landscape of Rhineland is a mixture of rocky outcrops, deep river gorges and meandering rivers, of quiet forests, luxuriant heathland and sun-drenched terraced vineyards. And everywhere there is history and legend, in the great cities, in the numerous medieval castles, and in many enchanting towns and villages that grace the banks of the Rhine, Mosel and other rivers of the region. Threading an undulating line along the wooded hills and ridges above the Rhine, between its villages, towns and cities, runs the High Level River Rhine Walking Trail, the Rheinhöhenweg, the subject of this guidebook.

THE RIVER RHINE WALKING TRAIL, THE RHEINHÖHENWEG

The Rheinhöhenweg, the "Rhine High Level Way", is a long distance walking trail which follows the course of the River Rhine from Bonn, the old temporary West German capital, upstream to Alsheim, a village deep in the heart of the famous Rhine vineyards, south of the city of Mainz. The total distance is 273km (169.5 miles). The trail, as described in this guidebook, can be walked in fourteen fairly relaxing stages and provides an opportunity not only to enjoy the outstanding scenery of the area, but also to visit some of the many places of historical, architectural and cultural interest in the Rhineland, deservedly the most famous of all the German regions.

Unlike the Thames Path in England, Britain's newest National Trail, opened in July 1996 and the first long distance path in the UK to follow the course of a river from source to sea, the Rheinhöhenweg does not faithfully follow the bank of the Rhine for its entire course.

Instead there are many sections which are several miles from the river and several hundred metres above it. This provides for a much greater variety of walking than might be expected from a river trail, the route reaching many high viewpoints* which offer extensive views of the river, its valley and the surrounding countryside of forested and open hillsides, heathland and vineyards. Consequently there is a moderate amount of ascent and descent on the trail but nothing too severe, neither in gradient nor length. The naming of the walk as a "High Route" is somewhat of a misnomer as it certainly is no mountain trail, the route basically traversing a long series of undulating, forested hills. The highest point reached on the whole trail is a mere 628m (2059ft) [on the Salzkopf, see Stage 9]. There is nevertheless a fair amount of up and down work as the route frequently returns to the banks of the river. In terms of severity the trail is more comparable to the Cotswold Way or the Cleveland Way than to the Pennine Way or the Cambrian Way - but there the similarity ends!

The majority of long distance walking trails in Britain and Europe avoid large towns and cities. The Rheinhöhenweg is rather different in this respect as, although for most of its length it follows paths through the countryside, through woods, heathland, fields and over hills down to numerous picturesque villages, it deliberately includes the large towns and cities in the region, in particular those of Bonn, Koblenz and Mainz. This allows the walking visitor to explore these fine cities and to visit cathedrals, churches, museums, etc, as desired. The walking through these cities is, on the whole, not unpleasant, but for those who dislike such urban walking there is always the option of taking one of the many local buses from the outskirts of the city to the centre, and another from the city centre to the point on the periphery where the Rheinhöhenweg can be resumed.

The other favourable difference between the Rheinhöhenweg and most other long distance paths is that whereas the latter usually traverse countryside where public transport is very sparse or non-existent, the Rheinhöhenweg, because it frequently returns to the Rhine valley bottom, which is served by an excellent train, boat and bus network, is well provided with public transport. Hence the walk is particularly suitable for those who wish only to sample certain sections of the Rheinhöhenweg. Also it is a simple matter to take days or half-days off from the trail to visit another valley, town or city,

*Note that *blick* = viewpoint in German. Placenames ending in *blick* are likely to offer good views. Many benches will be encountered along the route of the RHW, which often provide a chance to rest, relax and enjoy the view.

most of which are easily reached by public transport.

Another advantage of the Rheinhöhenweg is that it is well provided with accommodation of all categories and all price ranges, from hotels and pensions to youth hostels and campsites. Most towns and villages along the trail have tourist offices where English is usually spoken and where assistance in choosing and booking nightly accommodation can be sought. The only problems with acquiring accommodation may occur during the height of the summer season.

As the English translation of Rheinhöhenweg as the "Rhine High Level Way" is not a very manageable title, in this guidebook the trail will henceforth be referred to either by its German name, the Rheinhöhenweg, or by the abbreviation RHW.

There is in fact not one Rheinhöhenweg, but two. As well as the one described in this guidebook, which follows the left or southern bank of the Rhine, there is another RHW trail on the other side of the river, the right or northern bank of the Rhine. The author considers the Left Bank Trail to be the more interesting of the two, passing through more attractive countryside and visiting more interesting villages, but those wanting to sample the Right Bank Trail will find information on this in the "Epilogue" at the end of Stage 14.

The Left Bank Rheinhöhenweg starts its long journey south from the central railway station in Bonn, a few miles south of Cologne. From Bonn the trail passes through the elegant spa resort of Bad Godesburg to reach the town of Remagen which featured so prominently in the Allied advances of the Second World War. From here it skirts the lower regions of the Eifel range, passing through the towns of Sinzig, Bad Breisig and Andernach to reach the Mosel valley at the city of Koblenz, at the confluence of these two great German rivers, the Rhine and the Mosel. Here the Rheinhöhenweg crosses the other famous, well established, long distance path in the region, the Moselhöhenweg.

The second stage of the RHW leaves Koblenz to enter the Hunsrück, and soon it is traversing undulating, hilly countryside of forests and vineyards, above the most spectacular section of the River Rhine, the celebrated Rhine Gorge. The route passes through the picturesque medieval Rhine villages of Boppard, St Goar, Oberwesel and Bacharach to reach Bingen, passing many of the famous Rhineland castles en route. At Bingen the Rhine, which has until now been heading generally in a south-easterly direction, abruptly changes course to head slightly north of east for several miles, before once more swinging south-eastwards to flow through one of Germany's most elegant cities, Mainz. Forest now almost entirely gives way to vineyards as the last stages of the Rheinhöhenweg pass through the wine villages of Bodenheim, Nackenheim, Nierstein and Oppenheim to reach journey's end at the village of Alsheim.

The Rheinhöhenweg on its journey between Bonn and Alsheim passes through three German *Länder* or provinces, ie. Nordrhein-Westfalen (North Rhineland-Westphalia), from Bonn to near Rolandsbogen, Rheinland-Pfalz (Rhineland-Palatinate) from near Rolandsbogen to Mainz, and finally Hessen, from Mainz to the end of the trail at Alsheim.

It would be a pity to walk the RHW in its entirety without stopping for at least a day in one of the main towns or cities encountered en route, to enjoy a rest and some sightseeing. The two obvious places to spend such days are Koblenz and Mainz which, if reached after five and eleven days of walking respectively, as outlined in this guide, are well spaced for days off from the trail. There is much to see in both of these cities. If time is available there are many other cities, towns and regions that can be explored on and off route, and ideas for such excursions are given in the relevant sections of the guide. The Rheinhöhenweg can be walked in considerably less than fourteen days by fit and experienced long distance walkers, but to sample this route slowly, visiting as many places as possible en route, will provide the most satisfying walking holiday. The combination of walking and sightseeing is the ideal way to enjoy the Rheinhöhenweg.

EUROPEAN LONG DISTANCE TRAILS - THE E 8 AND THE E 3
There are at present eleven European Long Distance Paths, known as "E Routes", whose combined length is well in excess of 25,000km (15,500 miles). These international trails stretch from the North Sea to the Mediterranean (E 1 and E 2), to the Carpathians (E 8) and to Moscow (E 11); from the Atlantic to the Black Sea (E 3), to the Adriatic (E 5) and to Romania (E 7); from the Pyrenees to Lake Balaton (E 4); from the Baltic to the Adriatic (E 6) and to the Mediterranean (E 10). Not all of them are fully open at the time of writing and it will probably be well into the next century before all the waymarking is complete along their entire lengths. Moreover there are ambitious projects under consideration to extend several of them, including the E 4 southwards to the Peloponnese and the E 6 northwards through Scandinavia. The long term plan is to extend these E paths so that all European countries are linked to each other by a network of footpaths. The designation and establishment of these ultra-long distance footpaths is the work of the European Ramblers Association (ERA), an organisation, founded in 1969, which consists of some 40 walking

and mountaineering organisations in 20 European countries, representing some $2^{1}/_2$ million members. Wherever possible the aim is to designate already well established national long distance paths as part of the developing E Route network: this is the case with the Rheinhöhenweg in Germany.

The Rheinhöhenweg forms a small part of the E 8. This truly marathon route stretches from the Irish Sea (west coast of England) to the Rila mountains in Bulgaria, part of the Carpathian chain. On the way the trail passes through Holland, Germany, Austria, Slovakia, a small section of Russia, and Romania, a total distance in excess of 3000km (1860 miles). When passing through Rhineland the E 8 follows the Rhine for a considerable distance, using the Rheinhöhenweg from Bonn to a little before Bingen, a distance of over 160km (100 miles). The Left Hand Bank route of the Rheinhöhenweg, as described in this guidebook, is coincident with the E 8 for almost 70 percent of its length.

The really ambitious walker, with plenty of energy and time available, can reach the Rheinhöhenweg on foot from home by following the E 8. Firstly, the E 8 is walked across England from the Irish Sea at Southport to the North Sea at Hull. North Sea Ferries connect the UK stretch of the E 8 with its continental counterpart. Once in the Netherlands the E 8 route across continental Europe begins. From Amsterdam the trail crosses Holland to Nijmegen in the East, and then enters Germany at Kleve, continuing to Aachen and on to Bonn, where it picks up the Rheinhöhenweg, a trail distance of about 500km (300 miles) from Amsterdam.

The extension of the E 8, coast-to-coast across northern England, is the first European Trail or "E" route in Britain. This route, known in Britain as the Trans Pennine Trail, the most recent addition to the ultra-long distance E 8, was officially opened by Hubert Yseboodt, President of the European Ramblers Association, in July 1996.

The E 3 is another ultra-long distance international trail, which links Portugal, Spain (where it forms part of the famous Way of St James), France, Luxembourg and Germany, with Eastern Europe, a distance of several thousand kilometres. Only a tiny section of this cross-European trail, a mere few kilometres, is shared by the Rheinhöhenweg, in the vicinity of Bacharach (see Stage 9).

For more information on the E 8, the E 3 and the other European Long Distance "E" footpaths contact the European Ramblers' Association (see Appendix D for address).

CLIMATE - WHEN TO GO

The Rhineland of Germany has a climate not dissimilar from that of Britain, that is a temperate climate with rain possible at any time of the year. However, the area is situated several hundred kilometres inland from the Channel coastline and as a result the climate is more continental than that experienced by the British Isles. Summers tend to be warmer with generally more sunshine than in Britain (hence a climate more suited to the growing of wine grapes), whilst winters tend to be colder. The average daily temperatures for Frankfurt are 0°C in January and 21°C in July. Snowfall can occur at any time from November to the end of March, and winter days can often be quite raw. Hence most people would probably want to avoid winter for a walking holiday to Germany, although a snow-covered landscape is very attractive, and as the trees are without their leaves the views are often more extensive than during warmer months. Summer days can be quite hot but not generally of the severity experienced in southern Europe.

The best seasons for a walking holiday in the Rhineland are undoubtedly late spring and early autumn. Spring has the added bonus of a spectacular array of early flowers, with the many trees bursting into blossom and leaf, whilst birdsong is to be heard everywhere. The mellowness of autumn, with the rich reds, browns and golden yellow tints of the turning leaves, makes September and the first half of October a wonderful time to be in this part of the world, particularly because this is the season of the grape harvest, when many of the Rhineland villages hold wine festivals. Both in spring and in autumn, the problem of fully booked accommodation is far less acute than in the high seasons of summer, Christmas and Easter.

The climate is not the only consideration when making a decision as to the time of year to walk the Rheinhöhenweg. The area is a popular tourist attraction, and in particular seems to attract those people touring Europe by luxury coach. Great numbers of tourists during July and August can detract from the special atmosphere of this area, and can pose problems for those seeking accommodation, particularly on a nightly basis. The problem with the winter months is that, as in the UK, many of the castles and museums are closed during this low season (most of these establishments can be guaranteed to be open between Easter and October), so if visiting these attractions is a high priority for you do not visit the region between November and March. Some hotels and pensions are also closed during the main winter period, when their owners and managers take their own holidays. The Christmas and Easter periods have similar problems to

July and August, when accommodation tends to be fully booked.

In summary, the author would recommend either a late spring or early autumn holiday to walk the Rheinhöhenweg, but if you cannot be away from home during these periods then go anyway whatever the time of year - you are sure to enjoy it!

TRAVELLING TO THE REGION
There are four possible modes of transport from Britain to the Rhineland in Germany: by air, train, coach or private transport. When consulting timetables remember that Germany and its neighbouring countries operate CET (Central European Time) and so are one hour ahead of Britain throughout the year.

Air
The best airport to fly to for those planning to walk the Rheinhöhenweg is undoubtedly Frankfurt, as this is a major International Airport and consequently there are numerous flights connecting it to Britain's airports. Most of the main European carriers operate from the major British airports to Frankfurt, many with numerous and frequent daily services (in particular Lufthansa [German National Airlines] and British Airways). In addition many of the long haul carriers to Asia and Australasia, who commence their journeys in Britain, use Frankfurt as their European boarding airport so that often the plane is only partially full on this first, short leg of the flight and bargains can sometimes be had.

Frankfurt is close to Mainz, to which it is well connected by public transport. (The easiest way is to take a train or S-Bahn from the airport railway station to Frankfurt's main railway station, from where a train can be caught to Mainz.) From Mainz take a train or riverboat to Bonn to start the Rheinhöhenweg. At the end of the walk Frankfurt Airport is easily reached (on reaching Alsheim take a train back to Mainz and so return by train to Frankfurt Airport). All these services operate frequently.

Other airports to consider are Cologne, Düsseldorf and Mönchengladbach, although services from Britain are generally less frequent than to Frankfurt. Some of the budget airlines also operate to Frankfurt and neighbouring airports. Prices are generally competitive so be sure to shop around. APEX fares are available.

One disadvantage of flying is that the return home usually has to be booked in advance. Travel by train or by train and ferry (at least out of main season when advance booking is unnecessary) allows for greater flexibility.

Train

The introduction of the Eurostar Service between London (Waterloo) and Brussels via the Channel Tunnel has greatly facilitated travel to this part of Europe. At the time of writing there are two services a day from the International Terminal at Waterloo Station to Brussels Midi Station, but frequency is eventually expected to reach one an hour. The journey time is 3hrs 15mins but this time is likely to decrease when a new high speed line is opened in Belgium. From here it is about another 3hrs by express train to Cologne and on to Bonn for the start of the Rheinhöhenweg. Hence the train now is a serious contender for travel to this area of Europe. There are also direct services from the Midlands, northern England and Scotland. One obvious advantage of Eurostar over flying is that the train travels directly from city centre to city centre for ongoing connections. In terms of speed, cost and convenience the Eurostar train service will compete very favourably with the airlines, particularly for those living in the south-east of England.

There are also frequent but much slower services using express train and cross-Channel ferry. See Appendix D for the telephone number of British Rail European Enquiries. Further details can also be obtained from major British Rail Travel Centres. Train timetable information can be found in the Thomas Cook European Timetable, published monthly.

Coach

The cheapest way to travel to the Rhineland in Germany by public transport is by long distance coach. Eurolines, the arm of the National Express coach company operating to Europe, operates daily services from London's Victoria Coach Station to Cologne and Frankfurt, usually via the Dover/Calais ferry and Aachen. The journey time is a little over 11hrs. See Appendix D for the telephone number of National Express/Eurolines, but bookings can be made and further information obtained from principal National Express offices throughout Britain.

Private Transport

There are two disadvantages of driving a car to Germany to walk this trail. Firstly, the car has to be parked somewhere for the duration of the holiday. Sometimes it can be left in a hôtel car park provided a night or two is spent in the hôtel at the start and finish of the trip. Secondly, with a linear route such as this, public transport will have to be used anyway at the end of the walk to get back to the car left at the start. Nevertheless, the driving distance from the Channel or North Sea ports is not excessive and the route is generally on good, fast roads, so that use of the private car does warrant consideration, especially if it can be filled with three, four or more passengers, when this would undoubtedly be the cheapest way of travelling to the Rhine area.

There is a very extensive network of *autobahnen* (motorways) in Germany, which are very fast, efficient roads, but often of two lanes only. It is important to realise that although there is a recommended maximum speed limit of 130km/h on these motorways, this is not legally enforced so occasionally cars travel at very high speeds - be wary when using the fast lane. There are speed limits on other roads, however (usually 80-100km/h on country roads and 50km/h in built-up areas) and police operate radar speed traps with on-the-spot fines. Seat belts are compulsory on rear as well as on front seats. It is advisable to carry a red warning triangle in case of accident or puncture and to obtain a Green Card level of insurance. Travelling to the Rhineland will also involve driving through the neighbouring countries of Belgium, France, and the Netherlands, so the driver should accustom him or herself with the road network and traffic regulations in these countries before attempting the journey.

To reach the Continent there is the choice of using either a cross-Channel or North Sea ferry, or the Channel Tunnel. Note that the fare prices for taking a car on a cross-Channel or North Sea ferry vary considerably with season, day of the week and time of day. Be sure to check the price structuring outlined in the company brochures. See Appendix D for addresses and telephone numbers of the major ferry/hovercraft operators.

For speed and convenience there is little to beat Le Shuttle crossing by the Channel Tunnel. When fully operational Le Shuttle will operate trains every 15 minutes during peak times. From the M20 in Kent leave the motorway at Junction 11a to follow the signposts into the terminal at Folkestone. It is not possible to make a reservation for a specific train: simply turn up, buy a ticket at the tollbooths, proceed past customs and passport control before driving onto the train. The train speeds at up to 100mph; within 35 minutes you should have joined the French motorway network near to the village of Sangatte. When driving towards the Tunnel on the British side it is possible to check for any delays by tuning into Channel Tunnel Radio on 101.2 FM. Le Shuttle operates 24hrs a day, 365 days of the year. Further details can be obtained from Le Shuttle, Tel 01303 271100.

LOCAL TRANSPORT

Germany has one of the best integrated public transport systems in Europe. Trains, trams and buses are reliable, efficiently operated, clean and comfortable, although certainly the fares are not the cheapest in Europe! The Rheinhöhenweg follows the course of one of the principal communication networks in the country, the Rhine valley. Both road and rail hug the Rhine Gorge throughout its length. There are frequent express and local trains running along both the left and right banks of the Rhine, and frequent buses operate between the many towns and villages along the river and inland. In the cities encountered along the trail, such as Bonn, Koblenz and Mainz, there is a wide choice of urban tram and bus services. In addition frequent boat services operate between Easter and October, along the Rhine between Cologne and Mainz, and also along the Mosel between Koblenz and Cochem. There are also numerous ferry services across the Rhine, particularly in areas where road bridges are far apart.

The abundance, convenience and frequency of public transport along the Rheinhöhenweg allows for considerable flexibility. For example, those wanting to walk only a section of the trail can easily reach, by train or bus, most of the towns and villages through which the RHW passes, so can join and leave the trail at will with relative ease. There are many places of interest actually passed en route, but there are others which can easily be reached by a short local bus or train ride. The major possibilities for short or half-day and full-day excursions are discussed in the "Places of Interest" and "Summary" sections of this guidebook, with suggestions as to how they may be visited by public transport. Finally, the excellent public transport network in the Rhine valley can be used in areas where obtaining accommodation for the night proves difficult; simply take a bus or train along the valley to a town or village where a bed for the night can be secured, and return the next day. It is advisable to make the most of the excellent public transport that accompanies this route, for virtually no other long distance path, in Britain or abroad, is serviced with such good public transport. Further details of the public transport available in each area along the trail will be found under "Facilities" in each stage of the guide.

The train network in Germany is operated by the national company known as Deutsche Bundesbahn or DB for short. There are several different classes of train, from InterCityExpress (ICE), InterCity (IC) and EuroCity (EC) fast express trains, for which supplements are payable, to the slow local train (D-zug) which stops at virtually every station. There is often an efficient commuter train network within the cities, known as the S-Bahn, although these trains can become very overcrowded during the rush hours. It is worth investigating the various types of saver ticket, particularly those which are only available to foreigners. In particular it might suit the walking visitor to buy a German Rail Pass which gives unlimited travel for 5, 10 or 15 days (not necessarily consecutive) within a period of a month, on all trains, buses operated by *Bahnbusse* and on KD-Line Rhine steamers. This pass might be particularly useful to those wishing to combine walks along parts of the Rheinhöhenweg with a general sightseeing holiday in Germany. However, these train passes are expensive and would not be economical to those wishing to travel only relatively short distances on trains, buses or boats. Rail timetables can be purchased from major railway stations, or travel centres within Germany, all of which have good rail information centres.

Between Cologne (Köln) and Mainz, along the Left Bank of the Rhine, stopping trains serve the following stations, all passed through on the Rheinhöhenweg: Köln > Remagen > Bad Breisig > Andernach > Koblenz > Boppard > Bad Salzig > St Goar > Oberwesel > Bacharach > Bingen > Mainz.

Local buses, like the trains, generally operate punctually. There are a number of privately operated companies, but the DB also runs *Bahnbusse*, which are usually integrated with the train timetables. Note that there are no long distance coach services in Germany comparable to those which operate in Britain, with the exception of the international Eurolines services.

Rhine steamers are operated by the company KD-Lines, which stands for Köln-Düsseldorfer-Lines. Their vessels have such names as the *Loreley* and *Rheingold*. Although much slower than the local trains or buses, they offer an attractive, relaxing and often convenient mode of transport between the riverside villages, towns and cities of the Rhine. They can either be taken for an appreciable length of the scenic river, between, for instance, Mainz and Koblenz, either at the end or beginning of a walk along the Rheinhöhenweg, or else may be useful if a short journey along the river is necessary or desirable whilst actually walking the trail. Services are fairly frequent throughout the day during spring, summer and autumn, though it has to be said that standard fares are fairly expensive. There are offices and information kiosks of KD-Lines in all villages and towns along the river which the boats serve, often on the river bank at the landing stages. These all supply up-to-date timetable information, issue tickets or make advance bookings. Note that the most spectacular part of the Rhine Gorge (in terms of dramatic scenery and frequency of Rhine castles) is that between Bingen and St Goar, so those only wanting to sample a section of the river by steamer are advised to opt for a cruise along this section (see "Epilogue" at the end of Stage 14 for a further discussion on Rhine cruises).

General information on local buses and other public transport can be obtained from the numerous tourist offices in the region.

ACCOMMODATION: HOTELS, PENSIONS, YOUTH HOSTELS, CAMPING

Most walkers following the Rheinhöhenweg use hôtels or pensions as the basis of their accommodation. There is little shortage of these establishments in this holiday area. The main consideration is whether to book your accommodation before you leave Britain or whether to "hope for the best" in being able to find a bed each night. The former option is rather time consuming and requires you to make a decision in advance as to how far you are prepared to walk each day and where you wish to spend each night, although it does guarantee a bed. The second option allows you to vary the itinerary depending on the weather, the state of your feet (!) and the places of interest you find on the way, though at the expense of some sense of insecurity about where you are going to spend the night. The choice is yours, but your decision should above all be based on the time of year you are planning to walk the trail. In July and August accommodation is at a premium and fully booked hotels and pensions will be the norm. However, outside the main summer season (except for Christmas, Easter and German Bank Holiday periods - see "Public Holidays in Germany" below) finding suitable accommodation should not be a problem as there are so many hotels, pensions and private rooms in the area. (The author has been on a considerable number of European holidays walking long distance trails and has never booked accommodation before leaving home, but has never walked in the Rhineland during July or August.)

A sensible compromise would be to leave home without any secured accommodation (or perhaps having booked only for the first night) but, if it appears there may be problems later in securing accommodation, book it up as you go along, booking the next one, two or three nights in advance, either privately, by phone, or using the services of a local tourist office. If you do decide to book accommodation in advance from home, contact the Rhineland Tourist Offices (for addresses see Appendix D)* who will be able to supply

*Footnote: in the first instance it would be wise to contact the German National Tourist Office in London (See Appendix D - address 1)

you with lists of hotels and pensions. The Internet may also yield useful information. If finding accommodation when you arrive in Germany, the best option is first to locate the tourist office in each town (see "Facilities"); the staff will be able to provide you with information on types of accommodation available in the vicinity, and book a room for you. Be sure to tell them that you are on foot, otherwise they may book you a pension that is "only 10 minutes away" (by car!). The staff at these tourist offices are usually helpful and friendly, and most can speak English to varying levels of proficiency. It is always worth asking if there are any price reductions or other bargains available.

Hotels at most price ranges can be found in the area. There are perhaps more of the basic, relatively cheap hotel in Germany than in Britain, although the high star rated hotels are very costly. It is rare to find a hotel in Germany that is not clean and comfortable, albeit often somewhat formal and seemingly unfriendly. But in addition there are many pensions and private rooms offering B&B style accommodation. These are usually priced at around, or slightly above, their counterparts in Britain. They usually offer excellent value for money, often including a good buffet-style breakfast. When entering a town or village look for signs indicating "Zimmer Frei" or "Fremdenzimmer". Guesthouses (*Gasthäuser*) also usually offer very pleasant accommodation.

It is common for tourists in the Rhineland, most of whom are on travelling and sightseeing holidays, to require accommodation for just one or two nights, so the walker on the Rheinhöhenweg who only wants to stay for one night should not be at a disadvantage.

Germany was the birth place of the Youth Hostel movement, at the beginning of the twentieth century, and today there are many hostels throughout the length and breadth of the country. They are similar in character to those in Britain and a very popular form of budget accommodation in Germany, although unfortunately are often heavily booked by school and youth parties. Hostels are graded according to facilities and the dormitory / room size, and the grade of the hostel determines the price of the overnight accommodation. To stay in a German Youth Hostel (*Deutsche Jugendherberge*, often abbreviated to DJH) you need a membership card of a Youth Hostel Association recognised by the Hostelling International scheme (membership of the Associations of England & Wales, Scotland or Northern Ireland are all suitable). Or, you can join the German YHA or Hostelling International on the spot when arriving at a German Youth Hostel. Non-members are admitted, but at a somewhat higher overnight fee, and preference is given to those under 27 years of age. There are several youth hostels along the length of the Rhine (see Appendix A) but not enough to be used on every night whilst walking the Rheinhöhenweg. It is advisable to book ahead, if possible, during the main summer holiday season. For more information contact the German Youth Hostels Association (see Appendix D - Useful Addresses).

There are many campsites in the Rhine valley, often found on the banks of the Rhine itself, so they are easy to locate and often very convenient for RHW walkers. It is possible, as the author once did, to backpack the entire length of the Rheinhöhenweg using official campsites as the sole form of accommodation. Many of these camping grounds are large sites, with several facilities, often boasting an on-site restaurant, which is convenient for the lightweight camper who wishes to leave camp-cooking gear at home. It is possible to backpack the Rheinhöhenweg, carrying only a small lightweight tent, sleeping bag and insulating mat, but because the area abounds in restaurants, cafés and shops of all types which, particularly during the summer season, are often open late into the night and on all days of the week. The additional weight of a small tent, particularly if shared between two or more people, and a sleeping bag (which for summer use need not be a heavy 4-season) is relatively small. The abundance of campsites along the route, many of them offering excellent facilities in good locations, make camping a very attractive option. It goes a long way to solving the accommodation problem during July and August. Remember, however, that many of the Rhineland campsites are closed from October to Easter.

Walkers planning to camp wild on the Rheinhöhenweg should think again. The possibilities for wild camping are very limited; it is generally discouraged in most areas and illegal in many.

Finding campsites and youth hostels in Rhineland is relatively easy, as the recommended maps carry symbols which pinpoint their locations. Details of campsites on or near to the Rheinhöhenweg can be found under "Facilities" in each chapter, and further information is available from local tourist offices. Do not assume that the campsites mentioned in this guidebook are the only ones available on or near the trail; campsites, like all other facilities, come and go with time, so you would be well advised to consult an up-to-date campsite guide to Germany (or to the Rhineland alone). A selection of these publications is widely available in Germany, and some are obtainable in Britain from outlets such as W.H.Smith.

FOOD AND REFRESHMENTS; EATING OUT

One of the delights of a walking holiday in the Rhineland is the opportunity to eat out at several different restaurants. A great many will be passed en route, or reached by short detours. Standards in German restaurants are generally very high, with good quality food being the norm. Pork, prepared in a multitude of ways, is the most common meat. Chicken is also found on most menus. Sausages, of which there are a great many varieties, are very common, particularly when eaten as snacks. Most restaurants in Germany cater for vegetarians, with usually adequate choice. Both beer and wine, of course, are of high quality, and available everywhere. Breakfast is a much more filling meal than the croissants and jam of many continental countries, and is nearly always included in the price of a hotel room (buffet style breakfasts are common, with a choice of cereals, cold meats, cheeses, bread, jams, etc, with unlimited coffee or tea). Afternoon *Kaffee und Kuchen* (coffee and cakes) is almost an institution in Germany, and this pleasant snack can be taken in many of the cafés and restaurants along the trail.

If you prefer only a light lunch when on the trail there are many grocer's and baker's shops from which food can be purchased for a packed lunch; alternatively, on some days a café or snack bar can be found at a convenient point (see the "Facilities" sections). The snack bar or *imbiss* is common in Germany: snacks include sausages (of course!), chips, soups, sandwiches, etc, and are usually good value for money. There are many benches and picnic tables along the Rheinhöhenweg, usually with nearby litter bins (which are emptied regularly by countryside staff).

Perhaps the most important word to learn when travelling in Germany is *ruhetag*, which literally means "day of rest". Nearly all restaurants and cafés, and many pensions and guesthouses, have a *ruhetag*, ie. they are closed one day a week. The day of closure is decided by the owner and can be any day, so it is important to establish this to avoid disappointment. If you are staying in a town or village for two nights and visit a good restaurant on the first night, do not assume it will be open the following evening. Fortunately the *ruhetag* of most establishments is usually clearly displayed on the door (it therefore pays to learn the days of the week in German!). In areas where there are several restaurants, pensions, etc, it is common for different establishments to have different "closed days", so you should always find at least one restaurant open on any day of the week. It can on occasion, however, be distressing to arrive at the only restaurant or café for miles to find it closed!

There is little shortage of grocer's shops and supermarkets along or near to the Rheinhöhenweg, most selling a wide variety of good quality food. Check the "Facilities" sections for shops where food and drink can be purchased on each stage of the walk. A word of warning about Saturday afternoon shopping in Germany: it is common for most shops to close at lunchtime, so make sure you purchase sufficient food on Saturday morning to last you over the weekend. Also shops can sometimes be late opening on Monday mornings.

EQUIPMENT

Clothing suitable for walking in, say, the Yorkshire Dales or the Cotswolds is appropriate. However, remember that this is continental Europe and consequently summers tend to be a little warmer than those in Britain, whilst winters can be colder. The terrain is not particularly rugged or exposed to the elements, so full mountain gear is not generally required, although if walking during the winter do remember that severe weather conditions can be encountered.

Ensure that your pack is as light as possible. Nothing spoils a walking holiday more than the excessive weight of an overloaded rucksack. Be ruthless to ensure that no unnecessary items are taken. If making sole use of hôtel, pension or youth hostel, there is no reason why the pack should not be small and relatively light: this is neither a particularly long nor an arduous walk. *Remember, keep the weight down.*

The rucksack is probably the most important item of gear. Inspect it thoroughly for wear before leaving home and try to ensure that the carrying mechanism is not likely to break whilst on holiday. A dustbin liner and a supply of plastic bags will keep the contents dry in heavy rain. Equipment is best packed in different coloured stuff-sacs for easy identification and access. Perishable food is best kept in a disposable plastic bag.

A pair of lightweight boots is the recommended footwear, preferably well worn-in. Heavyweight mountain boots are most certainly not necessary. Some form of lightweight shoe is also a good idea for rest days, for relaxing in the evenings and for sightseeing. A pair of good quality trainers is recommended, as these can be used as alternative footwear on easy sections of the route during the drier summer months (though not during spring, autumn and winter, when some sections of the trail are muddy). Trainers are not a good idea when carrying more than a relatively light rucksack, as the risk of turning an ankle is too great. Remember to remove muddy footwear when entering hotels, pensions, restaurants, etc.

A windproof and waterproof jacket is an important item, to combat cold, windy, rainy days. As in Britain, spare warm, dry clothing should be carried at all times of the year. Several days of more or less continuous sunshine are not uncommon in the region during the summer, so remember to pack suncream, sun-hat, lip-salve and sunglasses. A small word of caution about wearing shorts: exposed legs (and arms for that matter) may be a target for ticks, which can carry nasty diseases. It is important to inspect exposed skin for these tiny beasts, or wear lightweight long trousers and long-sleeved shirts.

It is not necessary to carry large quantities of drinking water for most of the time when walking the trail, however, consideration should be given to the possibility of becoming dehydrated on a very hot day, and also out of season when some of the places of refreshment open during the holiday period may be closed. It is advisable to take along a water bottle or other container; one litre is more than adequate. Mineral waters sold in screw-cap plastic bottles are useful additional water carriers.

The backpacker will need to carry additional equipment, a small lightweight tent being the main requirement. A closed-cell type insulating mat is advisable to reduce loss of body heat through the ground. A sleeping bag in essential, although a lightweight one is probably adequate during the summer months.

If you intend to carry some form of stove, the most convenient type to use in Germany during the summer is the camping gas as spare canisters are readily available at campsites and shops. Methylated spirits and lead-free petrol can also be purchased. (If travelling by air, remember that none of these fuels can be carried on board.) Don't forget a small cooking set and lightweight cutlery, and matches or lighter.

Several miscellaneous items to consider are a small torch (useful in a tent or youth hostel) with spare bulb (best kept in the first aid kit to avoid breakage); a first-aid kit to treat minor cuts and bruises, blisters, headaches, etc.; insect repellent; a whistle for an emergency; a mini German/English dictionary or phrasebook; binoculars (for those interested in birdlife); camera; a Swiss Army knife or similar; small sewing kit; and a compass (useful, though not essential - see "Waymarking and Navigation" below).

MAPS
Maps at either 1:50,000 or 1:25,000 scale can be used for the RHW. The author recommends the 1:50,000 maps as they are quite adequate and

moreover considerably fewer maps are required, hence a significant cost saving.

Those walking the entire RHW are recommended the following 4 maps at 1:50,000 (in order from north to south [Bonn to Alsheim]):

Map 1: Naturpark Kottenforst-Ville (Südteil).
Map 2: Naturpark Rhein-Westerwald.
Map 3: Der Rhein von Bingen bis Koblenz.
Map 4: Mainz und Rheinhessen.

Germany does not have a widely known national mapping agency. Maps are produced by the individual *Länder* (counties or regions), so that obtaining information on the mapping of the whole country is not as easy as it is in Britain, for example. However the RHW traverses only three of the German *Länder* - Nordrhein-Westfalen, Rheinland-Pfalz and Hessen - and for most of the way is in Rheinland-Pfalz, so the problem is not a great one. Map 1 is published by Landesvermessungsamt Nordrhein-Westfalen, whilst Maps 2, 3 and 4 are published by Landesvermessungsamt Rheinland-Pfalz.

These four maps cover all but 5km (3 miles) of the entire route of the RHW from Bonn to Alsheim. The missing 5km are between Maps 2 and 3, between Andernach and Koblenz. However navigation in this area is not particularly difficult, and there is good waymarking on the ground along the section. Therefore most ramblers, with the aid of the detailed route description in this guidebook, and with due attention to the waymarking, should have little difficulty in following the RHW through this short mapless section.

Maps 2, 3 and 4 all cover appreciable lengths of the trail (see below), whereas Map 1 covers only 33.5km (20.8 miles) of the RHW and, more significantly, of this distance 21.5km (13.4 miles) are also covered by Map 2. Therefore only the first 12km (7.5 miles) of the trail, from the centre of Bonn to Bad Godesberg (Stage 1), are not covered by Maps 2, 3 and 4. Some walkers may therefore decide not to purchase the first map, but be warned that navigation can be complex in this early stage of the walk. Another option would be to substitute Map i) in the 1:25,000 series (see below) for the 1:50,000 Map 1.

Ramblers who have no wish to walk the entire trail but who would like to include a section of the RHW on their holiday will find the information below useful when deciding which maps to purchase

Map 1 - Naturpark Kottenforst-Ville (Südteil)
Covers the RHW from the start of the trail at Bonn to a point approximately mid-way between Calmuth and Remagen (Stages 1

and 2) ie. the first 35.5km (20.8 miles) of the trail. It overlaps with approximately 21.5km (13.4 miles) of the RHW on Map 2, below. Therefore only the first 12km (7.5 miles) of the RHW are unique to this map.

Map 2 - Naturpark Rhein-Westerwald
Covers the RHW from Bad Godesberg Railway Station to Kärlich (Stages 2, 3 and 4[part]) ie. from Km 12 to Km 78 of the RHW (where Bonn Railway Station is Km 0 and Alsheim Railway Station is Km 273). It overlaps with approximately 21.5km (13.4 miles) of the RHW on Map 1, above. Therefore 44.5km (27.68 miles) of the RHW are unique to this map.

There is a gap of approximately 5km (3 miles) of the RHW between Maps 2 and 3.

Map 3 - Der Rhein von Bingen bis Koblenz
Covers the RHW from Rübenach, west of Koblenz, to Jakobsberg, south-east of Bingen (Stages 4[part], 5, 6, 7, 8, 9, 10[part]) ie. from Km 83 to Km 201 of the RHW (where Bonn Railway Station is Km 0 and Alsheim Railway Station is Km 273). It overlaps with approximately 10km (6.2 miles) of the RHW on Map 4, below. Therefore 108km (67 miles) of the RHW are unique to this map. This is undoubtedly the best value for money of the maps covering the RHW.

Map 4 - Mainz und Rheinhessen
Covers the RHW from Bingerbrück to the end of the trail at Alsheim (Stages 10[part], 11, 12, 13 and 14) ie. from Km 191 to Km 273 of the RHW (where Bonn Railway Station is Km 0 and Alsheim Railway Station is Km 273). It overlaps with approximately 10km (6.2 miles) of the RHW on Map 3, above. Therefore 72km (44.7 miles) of the RHW are unique to this map.

If it is decided to opt for maps at a scale of 1:25,000, the following sheets will be required for the trail between Bonn and Mainz:

Map i):	Kottenforst und Drachenfelser Ländchen (alternatively the sheet entitled Naturpark Siebengebirge could be substituted for Map i).
Map ii):	Naturpark Rhein-Westerwald, Blatt 1 - West.
Map iii):	Naturpark Rhein-Westerwald, Blatt 3 - Süd.
Map iv):	Koblenz und Umgebung.
Map v):	Naturpark Nassau, Blatt 1 - West.
Map vi):	Naturpark Nassau, Blatt 4 - Süd.
Map vii):	Rheingau.
Map viii):	Wiesbaden und Umgebung.

There appear to be no maps at 1:25,000 easily available at present for the stretch from Mainz to Alsheim, so those opting for the 1:25,000 maps will still require the Mainz and Rheinhessen map at 1:50,000 (Map 4 above) to complete their walk.

Maps can be purchased from the outlets detailed in Appendix D (Useful Addresses).

Although these German maps are not of the same quality as British OS maps, they are nevertheless fairly accurate and easy to use. Furthermore, they are *wanderkarte* ie. specifically designed with the walker in mind, and have the route of the RHW (and other long distance paths in the area) clearly overlaid in red. Note however that the line of the RHW, as shown on these maps, does not always follow the waymarking of the RHW on the ground. The occasions where the two are in disagreement are highlighted here in the route description but also remember that with later editions of the maps, alterations, corrections and additional errors may be made, so be sure to navigate with care. If in doubt, after due reference to the map and to the route description in this book, always follow the RHW waymarking.

WAYMARKING AND NAVIGATION

Long distance paths in Europe are generally waymarked more thoroughly than those in Britain. This is the case in Germany.

The Rheinhöhenweg is waymarked throughout by the letter "R", painted on the boles of trees, on lampposts, walls, fences, etc. The most common form of this waymarking is a black "R" on a white background, sometimes accompanied by black direction arrows on a white background. The white background is usually an upright rectangle. However sometimes, rather confusingly, the waymark appears as a white "R" on a black background. Or very often the route is simply shown by the letter "R" crudely painted on a convenient surface, and occasionally there are purpose-built wooden signposts.

In several areas there are variants of the trail, or connecting links into towns and villages. These sections are waymarked as "RV", which stands for rheinhöhenverbindungswege.

Other trail markings will be seen on the walk. It cannot be stressed too strongly that only the "R" waymarks, or the "RV" waymarks where indicated in the text, should be followed, all others being ignored. These other waymarks are generally of two categories, ie. either depicting relatively short local walks, or other long distance trails. The majority are probably in the former category. Details of the numerous local trails, most of which are circular, can usually be obtained from a local tourist office. A common form of waymarking for local trails is a directional arrow accompanied simply by a number, eg. painted on a tree, this number relating to the walk number in the relevant local publication. Sometimes various symbols are used to waymark a local route, such as the "grape symbols" which mark the local walking trails around the vineyards in the St Goar area (see Stage 7).

Other waymarkings include the European Long Distance Walking Trails, or "E" routes (see "The E 8 - European International Long Distance Path" above); both the E 8 and the E 3 are coincident with the RHW in certain areas, but do not be lulled into following signs for these routes in case you miss the points at which the E trail and the Rheinhöhenweg diverge.

In the vicinity of Koblenz is the "M" waymark of the Moselhöhenweg (see Stage 5). The Rheinhöhenweg and the Moselhöhenweg are coincident for a few miles in the vicinity of Güls and Koblenz, so that in this region both the "R" and the "M" waymarks are followed, but be sure to locate the point at which the two long distance routes diverge (clearly indicated in the route description of Stage 6) and from then on only follow the "R" waymarkings.

In some areas, eg. the vicinity of Ohligsberg (see Stage 9) "IVV" waymarks will be seen. The IVV (internationale volksportverband or International Federation of Popular Sports) was founded in 1966 in Germany, and is today an extremely popular organisation in that country. Of the "popular sports" walking is by far the most widely practised by the IVV, which has now established itself in many countries, including Switzerland, Austria, France, Italy, Britain and Scandinavia. Walking events are organised throughout the year, but many "permanent waymarked trails", such as those seen along the Rheinhöhenweg, have been established. The IVV in Britain is represented by the British Walking Federation.

Although generally of quite an acceptable standard, the quality of the Rheinhöhenweg waymarking is perhaps not consistent. The author found the standard of waymarking to be superior south of Koblenz. It is well to remember, however, when searching for the next waymark, that waymarking is usually performed by teams of volunteers, most often from various local rambling clubs. Establishing, maintaining and waymarking the route from Bonn to Koblenz is the responsibility of the "Eifelverein" organisation, whereas south of Koblenz, the "Hunsrückverein" is the responsible body. In this guide particular care has been given to the route description in those areas where some difficulties may be experienced. However, areas that were once difficult to negotiate may not be so after the route has been re-waymarked, and this could happen at any time. Similarly, the loss of a crucial waymark can convert an easily navigable section into one of considerable difficulty. Waymarks in the larger towns are more prone to vandalism, and can be removed, defaced or, rarely, indicate the wrong direction. Pay particular attention in woodland where forestry activities frequently result in the loss of waymarks on felled trees. Occasionally new waymarks may indicate a slightly different line to the one indicated in this guidebook. In such cases the walker should, with due regard to the map, follow the new waymarking, making absolutely sure that this refers to the Rheinhöhenweg. On occasion a trail diversion sign may be encountered, when it will be necessary to follow the diverted waymarks until the guidebook route is rejoined.

It is advisable to carry maps and compass. A map is invaluable for naming neighbouring and approaching towns and villages on the way, or for making detours from the trail to find accommodation, food, or to visit a place of interest. A compass may be useful to help decide on the correct route when faced with two or more options, and for preventing the walker from going off in the wrong direction (a quick check with the compass will soon reveal the error). A compass also allows you to check the occasional magnetic or general bearings (eg. south-east, north-north-west) given in the text, and will certainly be an aid, when used in conjunction with the map, in relocating the correct trail if lost. It should be stressed, however, that navigation on the Rheinhöhenweg is not difficult. The route descriptions in this guide should be sufficient for you to follow the trail without problems. The golden rule is never to continue too far without seeing another "R" waymark. If one is not encountered for some time it is likely that the wrong path has been taken. It has been the author's experience that local people often stop to ask if you know the way, and frequently without being asked.

HAZARDS AND SAFETY
Walkers should be aware of the dangers of walking alone and decide for themselves whether they consider the risks acceptable or otherwise. Walking the Rheinhöhenweg is certainly no more dangerous than any popular walking region of the UK. Simple measures against petty crime are always advisable. Do not leave valuable items unattended in hôtel bedrooms, or in youth hostels or campsites, try not to leave gear in an unattended vehicle, and keep money, credit cards and passports on you at all times.

A warning should be given of the possibility of encountering ticks in the undergrowth of the Rhineland, particularly during the late spring and summer months; The problem is that ticks can carry bacteria and viruses which cause disease but this is fortunately rare. During the summer months, the skin should be inspected for ticks from time to time whilst walking in the Rhineland. If they become a problem then wear long trousers rather than shorts and avoid arm contact with vegetation where possible. If you find a tick take care in removing it as attempting to remove them with fingers or even tweezers may stimulate them to bury themselves into the skin. A trick used by some people is to smear a little Vaseline onto the skin at the point at which the tick has penetrated. This forces the beast to withdraw its head in order to breath, at which point it can be removed. However ticks, to my knowledge, are no more prevalent in the Rhineland than they are in other areas of Europe.

The walker in the Rhineland should also be aware of the dangers of bracken, which will be encountered occasionally, although not as much as in some areas of Britain. Apart from being a favourite habitat of ticks, the spores of the bracken plant are thought to be carcinogenic, therefore the wise walker will avoid contact with the fronds of the plant, particularly during the autumn when the spores on the under surface are in the process of dispersal. Walkers wearing shorts should be especially careful.

The possibility of falling victim to hypothermia is always a threat, particularly in the sometimes severe winters experienced in the region, and when the walker becomes wet during heavy rainfall and chilled by a biting wind. However the rambler is rarely far from the warmth of a hôtel, café or restaurant in this region. Steps should be taken on very hot summer days to avoid over exposure to the sun, resulting in dehydration and heat exhaustion, a potentially serious condition.

DOGS
Dogs can occasionally be a problem on the trail, particularly if they are unaccompanied. They are sometimes chained, but frequently on a long chain, so be sure to keep a good distance away from them. Never run or walk quickly past an unfriendly dog, as this may release its chase response. Walk slowly, backwards if necessary, facing the animal. Keep it in sight at all times but do not stare at the dog as it may regard this as a threat. More advice on how to deal with a potentially dangerous dog can be found in the leaflet "How should you cope with an unfriendly dog?" produced and issued free by the RSPCA

Statue and spring flowers in Bad Godesburg (Stages 1 & 2)
Konigswater on the right bank of the Rhine, seen in evening sunlight
(Stage 2)

The houses and church of Bad Bodendorf (Stage 3)
Leutesdorf and the River Rhine (Stage 4)

(send SAE to RSPCA, Causeway, Horsham, West Sussex RH12 1HG). If a bite is sustained, however slight, it is important to seek medical advice as soon as possible. Ask for an anti-tetanus inoculation unless such a jab has been acquired recently.

PHOTOGRAPHY

Some years ago the only type of camera worth considering was the 35mm SLR, preferably equipped with a wide angle lens and a telephoto lens - all very heavy. As the quality of 35mm compact cameras has become almost as good as the SLR, the walker can seriously consider taking a compact camera. The best type is one equipped with a medium zoom lens, but if a fixed lens camera is taken ensure that it has a reasonably wide-angled lens for landscape and townscape shots.

Both used and unused film should be protected from heat by keeping it well inside the rucksack. It is advisable to take all exposed film home rather than posting it back to Britain to be processed - it could be lost or damaged by X-ray equipment in the sorting offices.

LANGUAGE

English is the major foreign language taught in German schools and universities, and its global importance is well recognised by the Germans. There should be few language difficulties experienced in hotels, pensions, campsites, restaurants and large shops. In the large cities and towns such as Bonn, Koblenz and Mainz there will always be someone available who can speak English.

That said, some knowledge of the language will obviously enrich your experience of walking in Germany. Learning the elements of the language will definitely be beneficial, and consider taking a small phrase book to help out in restaurants and so on. The list of German words in Appendix B should prove useful.

MONEY AND BANKS

The Deutschmark (DM) is divided into 100 pfennigs (pennies). Banknotes are of 5, 10, 20, 50, 100, 200 and 500DM and coins are of 5, 10, 20 and 50 pfennigs and 1, 2 and 5DM. Eurocheques, travellers' cheques, credit and debit cards are all widely used in Germany. Mastercard and Visa are widely accepted and a useful form of payment for restaurant meals, hotel rooms, rail and boat tickets. However the use of credit cards in Germany is not as common as in Britain and many other European countries, so it is advisable to carry only the major worldwide cards.

Cash dispensers are found at most banks, and instructions are usually available in English.

An alternative method of obtaining local currency in Germany is to open a Girobank account in Britain and then request a Postcheque card and a book of Postcheques. These can be cashed easily in most post offices (no charge is levied). The Girobank account in Britain is debited after the documents reach Girobank headquarters.

As the Rheinhöhenweg passes through several large towns the walker will never be far from a bank, and exchange facilities for foreign currency and travellers' cheques can be found in virtually all banks. Banking hours are similar to those in Britain, most banks being closed all day Saturday. (For Bank Holidays see "Public Holidays in Germany".) Out-of-hours exchange facilities can often be found at main railway stations, and larger post offices will cash Eurocheques.

The EC currency (The 'Euro') will eventually replace the mark.

INSURANCE

Medical, and particularly hospitalisation, charges are very expensive in Germany so an adequate travel insurance is advisable. A good general policy designed for the independent traveller, obtainable from a number of reputable insurance brokers (see "Travel Insurance" in Appendix D) would be suitable, although it is always advisable to check first with the insurance company that your activities (viz. walking a long distance trail in Germany) would not invalidate a claim. Drivers are advised to obtain a Green Card level of insurance.

There are certain reciprocal rights available for British subjects in Germany under the National Health Service arrangements within the EU. Information concerning eligibility for medical cover under this scheme and the necessary E111 form can be obtained from local DHSS offices or from main post offices. It is not, however, advisable to rely solely on Form E111.

TELEPHONE BETWEEN BRITAIN AND GERMANY

Public telephones in Germany are a mixture of payphones and those requiring a phonecard. The walker following the Rheinhöhenweg will rarely be more than a few hours from a public phonebox.

If intending to make several phone calls whilst in Germany it is better to use a cardphone, so purchase one at the earliest opportunity from a post office, shop (newsagents and the like) or other advertised outlet. Remember that phonecards last indefinitely and so can be used on a subsequent visit to Germany. A call from a hôtel, café or restaurant is more expensive than from a public phonebox.

The procedure for placing a call from Germany to the UK is quite straightforward. Lift the receiver and insert the appropriate coins or phonecard. At the first dialing tone dial 00 (code for an international line), then at the second dialing tone dial 44 (code for the UK), then dial the STD code of the number required but minus the initial zero, then the number of the line required. For example, to phone a number in Birmingham (STD code 0121) dial: 00 - 44 - 121 123 4567.

If phoning Germany from Britain the code is 00 (for an international line) followed by 49 (code for Germany) then the individual number. The initial zero of the area, city or town code is omitted.

TIME IN GERMANY
Germany follows Central European Time (CET) which is one hour ahead of UK time. Both the UK and Germany change clocks on the same dates in March (one hour forward) and October (one hour back). So during the winter months Germany is at GMT + 1 hour and during the summer months GMT + 2 hours. The neighbouring countries of Holland, Belgium, Switzerland, Austria and France are also on CET and follow the same time changes as Germany.

PUBLIC HOLIDAYS IN GERMANY
Germany has similar, but not identical, bank holidays to those in Britain. Apart from 1st January, Good Friday, Easter Monday, 25th and 26th December, there is also 1st May (May Day), Ascension Day (changes annually - usually in May), Whit Monday (changes annually - in May or June) and 3rd October (Day of German Unity). Note that the *Länder* of Rheinland-Palatinate and North Rhineland-Westphalia take 1st November (All Saints Day) as a bank holiday, but that this is not a national holiday. Similarly Corpus Christi (changes annually) is taken in the three provinces Rheinland-Palatinate, North Rhineland-Westphalia and Hessen but again is not a national holiday. A few areas of Germany outside the Rheinhöhenweg recognise certain other annual holidays; these include 6th January (Epiphany) and 15th August (Assumption Day).

On bank holidays and certain annual festivals and holidays (of which there are many in the various regions of Germany) the public transport system can be considerably affected and many shops are closed, although most cafés and restaurants remain open. It is well to bear these days in mind and to plan accordingly, particularly if it is necessary to travel by public transport.

NOTES ON USING THE GUIDEBOOK

Layout of Guide

The Rheinhöhenweg Trail, from Bonn in the north to Alsheim in the south, has been divided into fourteen stages each of a day's duration. Each day has been designed so as to terminate at a place where there is some form of overnight accommodation, usually a choice of hotels, pensions and a campsite, and sometimes a youth hostel. In general the days are not long, although there is some variation in the length and severity of each section, necessitated by the need to reach suitable accommodation each night (see below). Other possibilities for accommodation along the route are also given and it must not be assumed that the daily itineraries described here have to be adhered to rigidly. There are several possibilities for decreasing the length of the various stages and lingering a while, or walking further each day if desired.

The first few days on the trail are relatively short and easy, to "ease" the walker into it. One of the major reasons for failing to complete a long distance walk is "overuse injury" (pulled muscles, extreme stiffness, severe blisters, etc) often sustained by attempting to walk too long and too fast during the early stages of the walk, when the body is unused to this type of exercise. You may walk regularly at home, say on one day most weekends, but in this case any minor problem you may develop will have disappeared after a week's break. However, on this type of holiday a minor injury sustained on the first day will be exacerbated by walking the following and subsequent days. The body has no time to heal itself. So for full enjoyment of the whole walk it is important not to attempt too much too soon, until you become "trail fit". Too many people see a long distance walk as an endurance test, to be completed as fast as possible. Relax and enjoy the walk; this is your holiday, after all. Keep the daily walking mileage down, allowing yourself time to visit the many places of interest passed along the RHW. Due to the abundance of accommodation on the first stages of the trail it is easy to walk relatively short stages, such as those suggested in this guidebook.

The central stages of the Rheinhöhenweg involve relatively long day walks. This is necessitated by the general lack of facilities, and particularly lack of accommodation, between the main centres of habitation. However, most ramblers will not find these stages long or hard, particularly as by this time you should be fairly fit and used to daily walking. Nevertheless, if these central stages become too arduous, an examination of the relevant map should show how the route may be shortened, or a way to deviate off the main trail to find accommodation for the night. Never be afraid to take a day off to rest if you are fatigued from walking day after day. Better this than sustain an injury which would curtail the walk completely. If you are tired after several moderately long stages by the time you reach Mainz, then the last three days offer short stages and easy walking, mainly through vineyards, with relatively few ascents and descents, during which time you can unwind, whilst preparing mentally for the return home at the end of your walk.

Prologue and Epilogue

There is so much to see and places to visit in this area that walkers may wish to spend a day or two on general sightseeing before beginning the Rheinhöhenweg, or at the end of the holiday. Ideas for "things to do and places to visit" at both ends of the trail are given in the "Prologue" in Stage 1 and in the "Epilogue" in Stage 14.

Table

Each "Stage" or "chapter" opens with a table providing distances, in both miles and kilometres, between the various places en route and accumulative distances for the entire trail. Major destinations are printed in capital letters. At these locations you can generally expect a wide choice of facilities: shops, accommodation, restaurants, etc. No "estimated times" are given to walk each section, but for those new to long distance walking the author would suggest that the "average" walker should allow about 4km per hour along most stretches of the trail, providing an unduly heavy load is not being carried, but this does not allow for activities such as stopping to admire the scenery, taking a photograph etc. Six or seven hours of walking per day is usually more than enough for most people. The summary table is followed by a number of sections subdivided under the following headings:

Facilities

Gives a summary of accommodation at the end of the stage, and often alternative stops en route and in nearby towns and villages, and information on hotels, pensions, youth hostels and campsites. Details of restaurants, cafés, bars, shops and public transport available during the stage are also given. This information will obviously change with time as establishments close and new ones open, so it should only be used as a guide to allow you to plan ahead for the next day or two with regard to food, accommodation and other services; up-to-date information is available from tourist offices.

Maps

The maps, at both 1:50,000 and 1:25,000 scale, which cover the day's walk are listed for easy reference. Most walkers will find the 1:50,000 maps adequate for the Rheinhöhenweg.

Places of Interest

Most walkers are "travellers" in the true sense of the word, not merely interested in putting one foot in front of the other, but have a desire to come to grips with the landscape, culture and history of the area at first hand. Many people like to combine walking with general sightseeing, particularly when in a foreign country. The Rhine valley not only offers excellent walking but is rich in places of historical and cultural interest. For this reason emphasis is given to items and places of interest both on and off route, with details of how they may be visited and incorporated into the walking holiday. This section describes towns, villages, castles and features of the landscape, plus occasionally other topics of interest to the Rheinhöhenweg walker such as other long distance trails encountered en route.

Summary

Offers a concise summary of the stage, describing the nature of the landscape and the features of the trail in the area, with particular emphasis on the highlights of the stage and "things not to miss". It would be particularly useful to read this section the night before walking the stage, to give a "flavour" of the coming walk and ensure that nothing of importance is missed.

Route

A detailed description of the route with special reference to potential navigational problems. Allowance should be made for possible differences in the route details and the current situation on the ground. Remarks such as "waymarking is poor in this area" relate to the time of the survey; things may have improved (or deteriorated!) since.

The aim of the route description is to prevent the user of this Guide from going astray whilst following the Rheinhöhenweg. Always use the route description in conjunction with the relevant maps and whilst following the waymarks.

References to "right" and "left" refer to the direction of travel when on the walk, ie. from Bonn towards Alsheim. However references to "right" and "left" banks of rivers and streams relate to their direction of flow. For example, if you are walking upstream on the left bank of a river then the water will be on your left, but if you are walking downstream on the left bank of a river the water will be on your right.

The route description at the start of each stage continues from the exact point where the trail was abandoned at the end of the previous stage. It is important to bear this in mind when leaving the route to finding lodgings for the night. Read the route description when continuing, with regard to "left" and "right" instructions, etc, as though you had walked through the town or village, without a stop.

Sketch map

A sketch map of the route is included for each stage. This is intended to be used in conjunction with both the route description and a relevant recommended German map.

Distances and Heights - Metric and Imperial

The length of each stage is given in miles and kilometres. The mileage was calculated arithmetically from distances in kilometres taken from the maps.

To avoid tedious repetition metric distances only (metres and kilometres) are given in the route descriptions. For example, if an instruction "turn left in 400 metres" is given, no conversion to yards or fraction of a mile is provided. This should present no problems if the description of the route is followed using the metric maps. Do not assume that given distances carry a high degree of accuracy. They are merely to give an indication of when the walker should look out for the change of direction: in a few seconds, a few minutes or much longer.

Heights are given in both metres and feet, the latter calculated arithmetically from data obtained from the metric maps. To avoid confusion the word "metre" denotes distance (eg. 400 metres), whereas "m" is used to indicate height (eg. 600m).

Miscellaneous Notes

The spellings of placenames used in the book are generally those given on the recommended German maps. The only exception to this rule is on the very few occasions where a signpost is encountered which gives a different spelling of a placename to that on the map. In this case the signpost spelling is given so there can be no confusion when reading the description of the route.

Road names in German can sometimes cause confusion if you are not conversant with the language. The word for road in German is Strasse. Sometimes this word is attached to the name of the road, eg. "Plonkerstrasse"; at other times the name and road are given as separate words, eg. "Plonker Strasse". In this guidebook the name is given as it appears on local road signs.

Guide

SUMMARY TABLE

STAGE	FROM/TO	DISTANCE	
		km	miles
1.	Bonn to Bad Godesberg	11.8	7.3
2.	Bad Godesberg to Remagen	23.5	14.6
3.	Remagen to Bad Breisig	15.1	9.4
4.	Bad Breisig to Andernach	15.6	9.7
5.	Andernach to Koblenz	26.4	16.4
6.	Koblenz to Boppard	23.5	14.6
7.	Boppard to St Goar	25.9	16.1
8.	St Goar to Bacharach	21.1	13.1
9.	Bacharach to Bingerbrück	27.9	17.3
10.	Bingerbrück to Ingelheim	16.6	10.3
11.	Ingelheim to Mainz	21.8	13.5
12.	Mainz to Bodenheim	13.8	8.6
13.	Bodenheim to Oppenheim	16.9	10.5
14.	Oppenheim to Alsheim	13.1	8.1
TOTAL	BONN to ALSHEIM	273km	169.5ml

PROLOGUE

There is a great deal to interest and therefore detain the visitor to this part of Germany, north of Bonn, the one-time capital of the former Federal State of West Germany, where the Rheinhöhenweg begins its long journey south up the Rhine. In particular, the beautiful city of Cologne (Köln), only 24km (15 miles) north-west of Bonn, and easily reached within 20 minutes by train from the latter, should not be missed by anyone who has not previously visited the city. It is suggested that a full day is set aside at the beginning of the trip, prior to commencing the walk, to visit Cologne, although most of its main

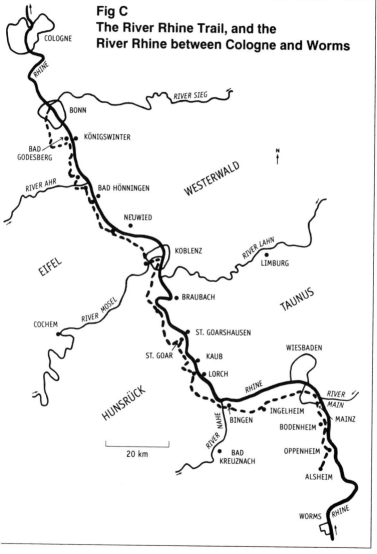

Fig C
The River Rhine Trail, and the
River Rhine between Cologne and Worms

COLOGNE

RHINE

RIVER SIEG

BONN

KÖNIGSWINTER

BAD GODESBERG

RIVER AHR

BAD HÖNNINGEN

WESTERWALD

N

NEUWIED

KOBLENZ

RIVER LAHN

LIMBURG

EIFEL

RIVER MOSEL

BRAUBACH

TAUNUS

COCHEM

ST. GOARSHAUSEN

ST. GOAR

KAUB

LORCH

WIESBADEN

RHINE

RIVER MAIN

HUNSRÜCK

INGELHEIM

MAINZ

RIVER NAHE

BINGEN

BODENHEIM

20 km

BAD KREUZNACH

OPPENHEIM

ALSHEIM

WORMS RHINE

41

attractions, which are conveniently situated close to both the main railway station and the River Rhine, could be visited in a couple of hours. Another option would be to visit the city by riverboat at the end of your walk, returning for example from Mainz, travelling up the Rhine as far as Cologne.

COLOGNE

Cologne is larger both in terms of geographical size and population (just a little under 1 million) than any of the towns and cities visited on the RHW; indeed it is the fourth largest city in Germany and the busiest in Rhineland. Situated on the left bank of the Rhine, this ancient city, founded by the Romans, boasts one of the most imposing Gothic cathedrals not only in Germany but in the whole of Europe. The twin spires of the building, whose foundation stone was laid in 1248 but which was not finally completed until over 600 years later, were at the time of their erection, in 1880, the highest man-made structures in the world (157m; 516ft). The Cathedral miraculously survived the Second World War largely unscathed. It contains a beautiful collection of stained-glass windows. It is possible to climb the 500 steps of the south tower for a very fine panoramic view of the city and the Rhine: to the south-east lies Bonn, your starting point for the long walk up the Rhine valley to Mainz and beyond.

There are several fine museums to visit in Cologne, the most notable of which are the Roman-German Museum (Cologne has some of the most impressive Roman remains in all Germany, including the superb Dionysus Mosaic, the finest in northern Europe) and the Wallraf-Richartz Museum which houses the city's collection of paintings. If at all possible try to visit Cologne during its prestigious pre-lenten carnival; you will not be disappointed.

Not everyone has found Cologne to their liking. The poet Samuel Taylor Coleridge, in particular, seemed to loath the place:

> *In Köln, a town of monks and bones,*
> *And pavements fang'd with murderous stones*
> *And rags, and hags, and hideous wenches;*
> *I counted two and seventy stenches,*
> *All well defined, and several stinks!*
> *Ye Nymphs that reign o'er sewers and sinks,*
> *The River Rhine, it is well known,*
> *Doth wash your city of Cologne;*
> *But tell me, Nymphs, what power divine*
> *Shall henceforth wash the River Rhine?*

Nowadays neither the city nor the river exude unpleasant odours. Hopefully you will enjoy your visit to the city before taking train or boat to Bonn, to commence walking the River Rhine Trail.

KEY TO MAPS

KEY TO FIG C
The River Rhine trail and the River Rhine
between Cologne and Worms

━━━━━	=	River Rhine.
━ ━ ━ ━	=	River Rhine Trail.
→———	=	tributaries of the Rhine, showing direction flow.

KEY TO RHEINHÖHENWEG SKETCH MAPS

━━→━━	=	route of River Rhine Trail with direction arrow.
▲	=	start and finish of each daily stage of the River Rhine Trail.
———————	=	other tracks and roads.
◄———	=	River Rhine, and other principal rivers, showing direction of flow, and positions of bridges and islands.
←———	=	other tributaries of Rhine, showing direction of flow.
·····□·····	=	railway with station.
●	=	city.
● •	=	towns and villages.
▲	=	summit or viewpoint.
•	=	other feature.

43

STAGE 1
Bonn to Bad Godesberg: 11.8km (7.3 miles)

LOCATIONS	DISTANCES			
	Sectional		Accumulative	
	kms	miles	kms	miles
BONN (55m; 180ft)	-	-	-	-
Venusberg (162m; 531ft)	3.2	2.0	3.2	2.0
BAD GODESBERG (122m; 400ft)	8.6	5.3	11.8	7.3

FACILITIES

There is no shortage of hotels in Bonn, and the tourist office (Münsterstrasse 20) will be able to supply a list of cheaper pensions. Cheaper still would be a night or two spent at one of the city's two excellent youth hostels, both of which are conveniently situated close to the RHW. The first is at Venusberg, almost halfway along this short stage; the second is in Bad Godesberg itself, at the end of the walk (see Appendix A for more details). The position of both hostels is shown on the 1:50,000 map. Campers will have to continue a little further on the RHW, along the Rhine, to reach Mehlem, where there is a large campsite, open all year, on the banks of the Rhine (see Stage 2).

There is adequate hotel accommodation in Bad Godesberg, which is almost a suburb of Bonn, but if any problems arise it is easy to catch a bus or train, or even boat, along the Rhine valley to find a hotel - maybe back to Bonn, or on to Mahlem, Oberwinter, Remagen or Sinzig. Buses run from Sinzig, Remagen, Rolandseck and Bad Godesberg about ten times a day Mondays to Fridays, but less frequently on Saturdays and Sundays.

Very many restaurants, cafés, bars, shops, banks and all the many other facilities of a substantial and important European city are, of course, all within easy reach of today's section.

MAPS

1:50,000: Naturpark Kottenforst-Ville, Südteil (Landesvermessungsamt Nordrhein-Westfalen).

1:25,000: Either Kottenforst und Drachenfelser Ländchen or Naturpark Siebengebirge (Landesvermessungsamt Nordrhein-Westfalen).

PLACES OF INTEREST
Bonn
Like Cologne, its larger neighbour, Bonn (population $1/4$ million) has
Roman origins, dating back to the Roman town of Castra Bonnensia.
It was the temporary capital of the Federal Republic of West Germany,
from 1949 until the early 1990s when the seat of government of a
unified Germany once more reverted to Berlin. Its other claim to fame
is its association with Beethoven, who was born there in 1770. His
birthplace, at Bonngasse 20, is now a museum devoted to Beethoven
memorabilia, a visit to which can be recommended.

Bonn's other museums include the Landesmuseum (Colman-
strasse 14-16, near the main railway station) and the Art Gallery of the
Akademisches Kunstmuseum, near the Hofgarten. The Schloss, built
in baroque style by the Archbishop-Electors of Cologne who originally
moved to Bonn in the thirteenth century, is one of the major buildings
of the city. Bonn has a relaxed atmosphere, far more provincial in
character than would be expected from a one-time capital, the reason,
indeed, why it was often known as the "Federal Village" when it held
the seat of government.

Poppelsdorf
An elegant suburb of Bonn, famous for its schloss or palace.
Poppelsdorf Palace, built in the eighteenth century, nowadays forms
part of the university, and is surrounded by the elegant botanical
gardens. Close by will be found Robert Schumann Haus, a museum
containing a number of artifacts relating to Bonn's other Romantic
composer. Schumann was mentally unstable, eventually attempting
suicide by jumping into the Rhine. Perhaps Schumann's most
celebrated symphony is that known as the "Rhenish" (Symphony
No.3 in E flat), a musical evocation of the river on which the composer
spent most of his life. Alas, the last two years of his life were spent in
an asylum near Bonn.

Kreuzberg
About a mile's detour from the RHW, lying to the west between
Poppelsdorf and the Venusberg and marked on the maps, will be
found Kreuzberg, like Venusberg, one of Bonn's many hills. Some
may find the detour worthwhile to visit the small isolated pilgrimage
church or chapel on the Kreuzberg, originally built in 1628, but

completely restored in Rococo style in 1746. The area is surrounded by the Kottenforst woods, one time royal hunting grounds.

Venusberg
Another of the hills of Bonn, to the south of the city and surrounded by attractive woodland. Venusberg marks the real start of the Rheinhöhenweg, once the city of Bonn has been left behind.

Bad Godesberg
A fashionable spa town, home of many of Bonn's embassies (including the British Embassy), and known for its many elegant buildings. Amongst these is the Redoute, built between 1780 and 1820. It was formerly a ballroom for the rich and socially conscious; nowadays it houses a fashionable and very expensive restaurant.

Bad Godesberg's claim to infamy comes from the fact that it was the meeting place of Hitler and Neville Chamberlain in 1938, which resulted in the "peace in our time" declaration, only a year before the outbreak of the Second World War.

The most imposing structure in Godesberg is its medieval castle, the most northerly of the famous Rhine Castles and therefore the first to be visited on the RHW, the first of many as you make your way southwards towards Mainz. The castle (Godesburg) was built in 1210, on a 122m (400ft) high hill overlooking the town, by the Archbishop-Electors of Cologne, but was largely destroyed at the end of the fourteenth century. The romantic ruins can be visited where an ascent of the circular keep can be made to obtain a view of the town, the Rhine and the surrounding countryside of the "Seven Hills".

SUMMARY
The "problem" with the RHW is that there is so much to interest the visitor along the way that it is often difficult to have time for walking! Indeed, even to get started on the trail can require considerable effort; as if Cologne hasn't delayed you enough then Bonn will almost certainly eat into the time available for the first day's walk. Fortunately the first stage is a short one, which should allow plenty of time to explore Bonn before leaving.

The Rheinhöhenweg starts from the main railway station (*Hauptbahnhof*) in the centre of Bonn. The cathedral is nearby, as is a smart pedestrianised shopping precinct from where food may be

Bad Godesburg Castle

purchased before setting out. The bus station is situated outside the railway station from where a bus may be taken to Venusberg if you wish to avoid a walk through the city. However, this walk through Bonn is quite pleasant and is a good way to see the city; if the route described here is followed it will not be long before the outskirts of this relatively small city are reached. The walk to Venusberg from the *Hauptbahnhof* takes approximately 1hr 15mins.

The walk out from the centre of Bonn offers an agreeable selection of town and leafy suburban walking, and a visit to the city university, after which the wooded hills and escarpment of Venusberg are the playground for the locals, many of whom will be seen strolling this delightful area on sunny Sunday afternoons. The stage ends in the elegant spa town of Bad Godesberg, home of many foreign embassies, the first of many charming riverside towns in which you will overnight on your journey south along the Rhine.

Today's stage will probably be enough for most people as a first day on the trail. Those carrying a tent, though, may like to consider continuing another 6 miles to Rolandsbogen, where there is a good campsite (see Stage 2).

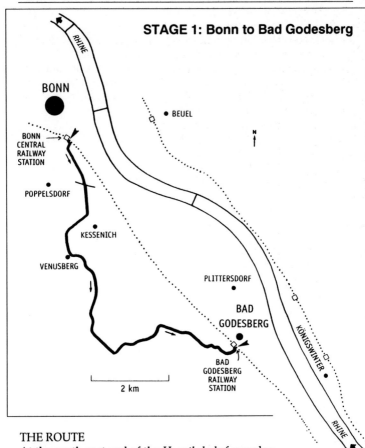

STAGE 1: Bonn to Bad Godesberg

RHINE

BONN

BONN CENTRAL RAILWAY STATION

POPPELSDORF

KESSENICH

VENUSBERG

BEUEL

N

PLITTERSDORF

BAD GODESBERG

BAD GODESBERG RAILWAY STATION

KÖNIGSWINTER

RHINE

2 km

THE ROUTE
At the south-east end of the *Hauptbahnhof* complex
seek out a pedestrian subway which passes under
the railway lines (marked as Poppelsdorfer Allee 15). Take this
underpass and then walk along Poppelsdorfer Allee, under an avenue
of trees with a large grassy area to your right. At the first crossroads
turn left onto Bonner Talweg. Remain on this road heading south-
east to cross Weberstrasse and several other smaller streets to enter
the suburb of Poppelsdorfer. Cross the main road of Reuterstrasse to

enter the suburb of Kessenich and keep ahead on Bonner Talweg. Continue ahead at a large roundabout, still on Bonner Talweg. Where the latter ends bear left onto Lotharstrasse, heading for the church spire which is clearly visible. Before reaching it turn right onto Rosenburgweg, now beginning the first gentle ascent of the walk. Soon ignore two roads on the right, but instead continue ahead on the Rosenburgweg as it climbs, swinging first to the left and then to the right. When the gradient increases somewhat the surface of the lane deteriorates as the route becomes a *Waldweg* (forest trail) on which motorised traffic is prohibited. The climb ends at a cross-tracks in the woods. Bear left here to pass a large stone monument on your left to Kaiser Wilhems I. Head south over the Rosenburg to reach the Hauweg and a main road at the Steigenberger Hotel on the outskirts of Venusberg.

Turn left onto the main road (Robert-Koch-Strasse). Walkers intending to stay at the youth hostel should follow the signpost for *Jugendherberge* to the right along Haager Weg, but for the RHW remain on the main road. A few metres after a bus stop* look for the green waymarks on a lamppost which indicate Walking Route No.1 - Eifelverein Haupt-Wanderweg and the Rheinhöhenweg (the first "R" waymark of the trail). Both these routes take the *Waldweg* footpath on the left: within 50 metres turn right following the "R" waymarks along a woodland path which runs parallel to Robert-Koch-Strasse, which is over to your right. When the path emerges onto a lane walk ahead, passing to the left of the University Clinic to enter a nature reserve. Pass over a bridge at the Dienstweg to continue on the woodland track ahead. Pass a bench at a viewpoint of the Rhine valley. The track follows a stone wall for a while to reach a circular wooden shelter in the woods. Take the track passing immediately to the right of this shelter, heading south. Continue ahead at a 5-way cross-tracks.

Continue to a T-junction at a narrow metalled lane; here turn left, heading downhill towards the south. Pass another circular wooden shelter, this time on your right, and after this a stone, also on your right, on which is a waymark (rather faded) indicating the way to the right to "Waldau Wildpark" in 20mins. Ignore this waymark, but remain on the forest track ahead which soon swings sharply to the left

* Those taking the bus from the centre of Bonn should alight here in Venusberg. It takes about 1hr 15mins to walk to this point from the centre of Bonn.

to pass over a (usually) dried-up forest stream. The way now heads to the south-east, with woods to the left and open fields to the right. Remain ahead on the *Waldweg* at the next cross-tracks. At the far end of a pond on the right-hand side of the track there is a bifurcation of ways: Route No.1 and one variant of the E8 (black triangle waymarks) take a track on the right, whereas we turn left (ignore the E8 waymarks ahead) on a woodland path heading north-east. After about 350 metres, at the next path on the right, turn right along it (bearing 100 degrees magnetic). In a further 250 metres turn left at a path/track junction, now heading downhill on a track (bearing 50 degrees magnetic). However, within 50 metres turn right off this main track, downhill on a footpath ("R" waymark easily missed). Descend on this path eastwards to reach a flight of broadly spaced steps which lead down to a track (stream and gully on the right). Turn right on the track to follow it round a left-hand bend, and continue now with the stream on your left.

The track heads north-eastwards, then northwards and then, on reaching the edge of the escarpment above the Rhine valley, swings to the right to descend east-south-east. On reaching a road continue ahead (east) along the Promenadeweg. The turret of Godesburg Castle is soon seen on the hill ahead. When the metalled road comes to an end take the right (higher) of the two footpaths ahead, climbing into the Bad Godesberg Woods. Climb to reach Am Burgfrienhof, bearing left downhill on this lane. Continue to a T-junction where you turn left on Winterstrasse for 60 metres and then left again on Auf dem Godesberg. Where this lane swings sharply to the left uphill, turn right on a paved drive ("Innenstadt" signpost) downhill. Later bear right at an old stone cross (only the hands and feet of Christ remain) to descend a flight of steps to cross a footbridge over a main road. Cross a pedestrianised area (Michael Platz) in the heart of the town of Bad Godesberg.

Cross a main road (Am Kurpark) and bear left through the small park, following "RV" waymarks ("RV" is an abbreviation of Rheinhöhen - Verbindungsweg). Cross the Koblenzer Strasse and continue through the park to reach Bad Godesberg railway station.

STAGE 2
Bad Godesberg to Remagen: 23.5km (14.6 miles)

LOCATIONS	DISTANCES			
	Sectional		Accumulative	
	kms	miles	kms	miles
BAD GODESBERG (122m; 400ft)	-	-	11.8	7.3
Rüngsdorf (left bank of Rhine)	2.5	1.6	14.3	8.9
Mehlem	4.5	2.8	18.8	11.7
Rodderberg				
(Heinrichs Blick - 160m; 525ft)	1.4	0.9	20.2	12.6
Rolandsbogen	0.9	0.5	21.1	13.1
Rolandseck	2.1	1.3	23.2	14.4
Berschberg (195m; 639ft)	1.8	1.1	25.0	15.5
Waldheide	1.1	0.7	26.1	16.2
Birgel	0.9	0.6	27.0	16.8
Birgeler Kopf (177m; 580ft)	0.6	0.3	27.6	17.1
Unkelbach	2.2	1.4	29.8	18.5
Calmuth	2.2	1.4	32.0	19.9
Apollinariskirche (church)	2.7	1.7	34.7	21.6
REMAGEN (55m; 180ft)	0.6	0.3	35.3	21.9

FACILITIES

There are several hotels in Remagen, as well as cheaper pension and B&B type establishments; the tourist office in Bachstrasse should be able to help. There are also a few hotels and pensions in the towns and villages between Bad Godesberg and Remagen.

There is no youth hostel accommodation on the left bank of the Rhine, but there is a hostel in Bad Honnef, on the right bank (see Appendix A).

Campers will find a convenient campsite on the shore of the Rhine at Remagen. There is also a campsite at Rolandsbogen on the banks of the Rhine, opposite the island of Nonnenwerth and, a kilometre further north, another at Mehlem, also by the Rhine.

Numerous shops, restaurants, cafés and a bank will be found in Remagen.

En route there is a restaurant at Rolandsbogen and a guesthouse/café a little before the Apollinariskirche.

MAPS

1:50,000: Naturpark Rhein-Westerwald (Landesvermessungsamt Rheinland-Pfalz) covers the whole route. Naturpark Kottenforst-Ville, Südteil (Landesvermessungsamt Nordrhein-Westfalen) covers all but the last 2km (1.2 miles) of the section.

1:25,000: Either Kottenforst und Drachenfelser Ländchen or Naturpark Siebengebirge (Landesvermessungsamt Nordrhein-Westfalen) plus Naturpark Rhein-Westerwald, Blatt 1 - West (Landesvermessungsamt Rheinland-Pfalz).

PLACES OF INTEREST

Siebengebirge

The "Seven Hills" or "Mountains" are all on the eastern side of the Rhine, in view for a considerable distance whilst walking the RHW along the left bank in this area. Although only 320-460m (1050-1508ft) in height, the hills, of which there are many more than seven in number, stand proud of the Rhine plain and form a well-recognised feature of the region's topography. Legend has it that their origin is related to the work of seven giants who, working with seven spades, cleared the immense mountains in the area, so freeing the Rhine to flow on its course. Having finished their work they shook off the remaining earth from their spades, so creating the Seven Hills.

The main summits in this wooded range of hills are the Grosse Olberg (460m; 1508ft), Löwenburg (455m; 1492ft), Lohrberg (435m; 1426ft), Nonnenstromberg (335m; 1098ft), Petersberg (331m; 1085ft), Wolkenburg (325m; 1065ft) and Drachenfels (321m; 1052ft), but of the seven the latter and lowest is by far the most well known (see below). For many centuries these hills were intensely quarried for stone, principally the minerals trachyte, basalt and dolerite, all used for local building purposes. However, a powerful environmental conservation lobby, operating as far back as the late nineteenth century, stopped all this commercial exploitation, forming what became Germany's first National Park. The area today is still well protected and is very popular with local ramblers, who are much in evidence at weekends. If time is available take a day-off from the RHW to explore this area.

Drachenfels

The "Dragon's Rock" is the most well known and popular of the Siebengebirge, a centre of Romantic Rhine folklore. According to the Nibelung legends Siegfried killed the dragon who lived there, then bathed in the spilled blood to give him invincibility. The summit can be reached by a tourist railway or, much better, by a path that passes the Dragon's lair on the way up! There are many cafés in the area. At the top are the ruins of Drachenfels Castle, built in the early twelfth century by the Archbishop of Cologne, but slighted during the Thirty Years War. The poet Lord Byron came here, penning the famous lines:

> *The castle crag of Drachenfels*
> *Frowns o'er the wide and winding Rhine.*

in his epic poem *Childe Harold's Pilgrimage*.

On nearby slopes some of the grapes are used to produce wine known as Dragon's Blood (Drachenblut).

Königswinter

A popular resort on the right (east) bank of the Rhine. RHW walkers will need to take a ferry across the river in order to visit the town, which is a good base from which to explore the Siebengebirge. Its name might imply that it was once the winter residence of kings and emperors, but this is false, as the name comes from the word *Vintra* meaning vineyards.

Bad Honnef and Rhöndorf

Bad Honnef is another fashionable spa town, but being on the right bank it does not suffer from the encroachment of Bonn, as does Bad Godesberg on the left bank. Patients come here in search of relief from rheumatism. Bad Honnef is a pleasant place in which to stroll. Its neighbouring town, Rhöndorf, was the home of Adenauer, the first Chancellor of the Federal Republic. His house is now a museum (Adenauer Strasse 8c) containing an abundance of memorabilia.

Rolandsbogen

The area is associated with the soldier "Roland", nephew of Charlemagne, who was killed by the Basques in the Pyrenees during the invasion of Spain, so becoming the hero of the eleventh century *Chanson de Roland* (Song of Roland). His betrothed, Hildegard, lived in this region, but on hearing of his death immediately took Holy Vows, retreating to the convent on the island of Nonnenwerth in the

Rhine, opposite Rolandsbogen. The legends are confused because Roland seems to have come miraculously back to life to spend the rest of his days at Rolandsbogen, so close and yet now unavailable to Hildegard. All that now remains of the castle fortress of Rolandsbogen, originally built in the eleventh century, is an ivy-covered stone arch on a hill-top overlooking the Rhine (the name Rolandsbogen in fact means Roland's Arch). There are superb views from the ruins of the Rhine, the "Seven Hills" and the surrounding resorts. The Rolandsbogen restaurant is famous as the venue for the engagement party of Konrad Adenauer in 1902.

Rolandseck
The disused railway station at Rolandseck is well known amongst the German avant-garde as a cultural centre and gallery of modern art (the Künstlerbahnhof).

Oberwinter
Oberwinter is a small town situated on the left bank between Rolandseck and Remagen. Its name means "above the vineyards".

Unkel
A pretty town on the right bank, seen from the RHW. It is famous for its autumn wine festivals, and for the fact that Beethoven was supposed to have been locked up for the night in one of the towers of the town ramparts, after being unable to pay his bill at a local tavern.

St Apollinaris Church (Apollinariskirche)
Standing high above the town of Remagen this large, attractive, neo-Gothic pilgrimage church dates from the mid-nineteenth century, when it was constructed by the architect also responsible for the famous Dom in Cologne. The RHW conveniently passes the building. Inside there are many frescos on the walls depicting scenes from the lives of Christ, the Virgin and St Apollinaris, a saint not too well known, except here at Remagen.

Remagen
Remagen has ancient origins, being known in Roman times as Rigomagus, but within modern history it is, of course, mainly known for its bridge - which incidentally is no longer here! The bridge across

the Rhine at Remagen was built during the First World War on the orders of General Ludendorff, but its claim to fame came in the Second World War thirty years later. It was captured intact by a group of American soldiers in March 1945, so allowing the first Allied bridgehead to be established on the eastern side of the Rhine. Some days afterwards the bridge collapsed, killing several American soldiers. After the War the bridge was never rebuilt, but the large towers on the banks of the river remain. These now house museums, the one on the Remagen side relating the history of the bridge.

Also of interest in Remagen is the Basilica of St Peter and St Paul, enlarged at the beginning of this century and near to the Roman gateway of the Pfarrhoftor, which is decorated with relief sculptures.

SUMMARY
At last the River Rhine is actually encountered for the first time since leaving Bonn! The day starts with a walk through Bad Godesberg to reach the left bank. Then follows a very pleasant riverside walk for over 2 miles, with majestic views of the river and the Siebengebirge beyond, and across to fashionable Königswinter on the right bank, which could be visited by river ferry by those with time available. (However, don't spend too much time on detours as the walk today is reasonably long).

After this section of flat, easy walking, the route takes to the gentle hills to the west of the river, the Rodderberg and Rolandsberg ranges. The country is undulating, with a fair amount of ascent and descent, but nothing too strenuous. There are three principal hills, all of which offer excellent viewpoints of the Rhine and the Siebengebirge to the east. First comes Rodderberg, where the Heinrich's viewpoint (Heinrichs Blick) is perhaps the finest of the day. Then follows the slightly higher Berschberg, and finally the Birgeler Kopf less than half a kilometre from the left bank but over 120m above it. More undulating country continues as the route passes through the village of Unkelbach and later Calmúth, before the RHW reaches one of its gems, the impressive neo-Gothic church of St Apollinaris, which stands high above the river and the historically significant town of Remagen, where there is plenty of opportunity for overnight accommodation and much to interest the visitor.

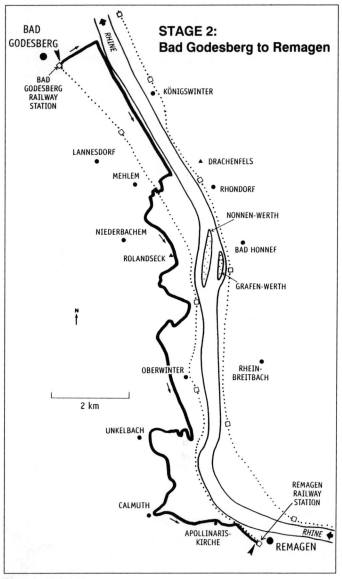

STAGE 2:
Bad Godesberg to Remagen

BAD GODESBERG

RHINE

BAD GODESBERG RAILWAY STATION

KÖNIGSWINTER

LANNESDORF

DRACHENFELS

MEHLEM

RHONDORF

NONNEN-WERTH

NIEDERBACHEM

BAD HONNEF

ROLANDSECK

GRAFEN-WERTH

N

OBERWINTER

RHEIN-BREITBACH

2 km

UNKELBACH

REMAGEN RAILWAY STATION

CALMUTH

RHINE

APOLLINARIS-KIRCHE

REMAGEN

THE ROUTE

From Bad Godesberg railway station turn left down Rüngsdorfer Strasse, bearing right after 200 metres to pass under the railway lines. Continue ahead on Rheinallee, following "RV" waymarks. Walk ahead at the next crossroads, still following Rheinallee. Pass the Pakistan, Ghana and Cameroon embassies and then cross the Ubierstrasse. A hundred metres later cross the Basteistrasse and take the "RV" waymarked footpath across the park to reach the banks of the river. Turn right to follow the left-hand bank for almost 4km. There is a separate foot and cycle path alongside the river, providing easy, relaxed walking with lovely views of the wide river, passing barges and the wooded hills dotted with châteaux that rise above the opposite bank. The route passes the attractive riparian resort of Königswinter on the opposite shore of the Rhine: this town can be visited by ferry.

When opposite the centre of Königswinter, 2.4km after joining the river, the trail crosses a road to continue along the shore of the Rhine for a further 1.4km. About 250 metres after the landing stage for the Siebengebirgs Line, turn right on a footpath through a grassy area. Cross a minor road and continue ahead with a large grassy area to your right. Climb a short flight of steps to reach a road (Mainzer Strasse). Turn left along this road for 250 metres to the traffic lights at Hagenstrasse. Turn right along the latter to pass under a road and then railway lines to reach another set of traffic lights. Here turn left and then first right onto Oberaustrasse, which soon becomes a narrow metalled footpath that climbs steeply to reach Rodderbergstrasse. Turn left along this leafy lane. After 200 metres turn right onto Elsternweg. Climb on this road until it ends to become a footpath. Continue the climb on this path and keep ahead at a cross-tracks. At a track T-junction turn left continuing to climb gently to meet a metalled lane. Turn left onto this lane to traverse the Rodderberg, with superb views left down to the Rhine and over to the hills in the north-east. There are seats at Heinrichs Blick to relax and admire the view. The area is a nature reserve.

Soon after Heinrichs Blick the trail passes into Rheinland Pfalz Länder. Remain on this peaceful lane, later following the signpost to Rolandsbogen. The RHW bears right at the sign for the Rolandsbogen Restaurant (*). However, those walkers wanting the campsite or other accommodation in the valley should continue ahead downhill at this point, following the sign for Rolandsbogen (this detour down to the Rhine near Rolandseck is now described; for the continuation of the RHW description skip to ** below). The track descends steeply to pass under a stone bridge. Follow "RV" signs on a path that descends beneath a second stone bridge. Continue the steep descent to pass under a third bridge (concrete) to emerge at the main road in front of the Rhine. Turn left for about 900 metres to reach the campsite. Frequent buses (less frequent at weekends) pass along this road between Sinzig, Remagen and Bad Godesberg, places which all have a good selection of accommodation.

(**) Continued from (*) above. After passing the sign for the Rolandsbogen Restaurant ignore a left turn signposted to Rodderberghof, but instead remain ahead on the lane. When the road swings sharply to the right, walk ahead on a footpath/narrow track, entering a nature reserve (NB. keep strictly to the waymarked route in this region). After a few hundred metres, at a Y-junction, take the left-hand branch. The trail soon descends in a wide arc round the head of a woodland valley. Descend to a small lake on your right: turn right at the track T-junction here to climb past the lake. A few metres after the far end of the lake turn left onto another earthen track. Bear right at the next track junction and 60 metres later turn right again at a path T-junction. Pass through an open area (trees newly planted in 1995) and, at its far end, ignore a "RV" waymark going left, but keep instead to the "R" marked trail bending to the right. Keep to the main track to reach a circular wooden shelter at a Y-junction: take the left branch here in front of the shelter. Follow this trail heading towards Birgel, always keeping to the main track, ignoring any side turnings to left and right. The forest track eventually emerges at a road by a small roundabout: continue ahead along this road, magnetic bearing 165 degrees.

Descend to a road junction where you walk ahead into Birgel (ignore the "RV" route along Oelbergweg on the left). Follow the signposts for the Rheinhöhenweg ahead. Continue ahead at a crossroads where there is a cross dated 1723, but 150 metres after be sure to turn right at a small crossroads. On reaching a barbed fence (military installation) take the footpath to its left, alongside a low wall. Climb to the summit of Birgel Kopf before descending on a narrow waymarked path through woodland. There are views down to the Rhine on your left. Follow the "R" waymarks carefully down a series of narrow woodland paths and a gully to emerge at a road. Walk ahead along this for 200 metres to the lane on the left, viz. Am Busenberg. Turn left on this road for only 20 metres before turning left along a narrow, grassy footpath, which has a bank to its right. Follow this footpath, eventually crossing a small concrete footbridge over a stream to reach the high street of the village of Unkelbach (church and village centre to the right).

Turn left for 20 metres and then right along Wiesenstrasse. Cross straight over Rheinstrasse to follow the surfaced track ahead: continue ahead at a cross-tracks, now on an unsurfaced grassy track. In 100 metres or so ignore a track on the left, but continue ahead, aiming for the wood. The trail climbs into the wood, heading east for a while

Religious monument passed on the trail above Apollinariskirche, near Remagen

59

before resuming a southerly direction. Bear left on reaching a forest track for about 100 metres, before turning right off this onto a narrow "R" waymarked woodland path. This path leads to a track at a hairpin bend: continue ahead on the left (lower) branch of this track. The trail descends to a narrow metalled lane: turn right along this for about 600 metres to a point where there is a barrier on the road. Turn left onto a forest track here (building on the left), but after only 5 metres (ie. before the building) turn sharp left onto a woodland path heading eastwards. Within a further 100 metres take the right fork at a Y-junction, climbing into the woods. Climb to a track T-junction where you turn left. Keep to the right at the next Y-junction and later ignore another track off to the right. Bear right at yet another Y-junction to reach a barrier just before a metalled lane. Turn left onto a footpath which starts 10 metres before the road. The path runs parallel with the road for a while before bearing left to pass behind some buildings. Pass to the right of a large pond to emerge at the road by a guesthouse/café (note the interesting gnome garden on the right). [NB. this is the point where the Rheinhöhenweg leaves the 1:50,000 map entitled "Naturpark Kottenforst-Ville, Südteil". The remainder of this stage is covered on the 1:50,000 sheet entitled "Naturpark Rhein-Westerwald"].

Turn left onto the road for 50 metres and then take the narrow footpath on the left between a track and the road: Turn left at a track T-junction and 50 metres later ignore another track on the right. The trail leads to a large religious stone monument at a viewpoint in front of a church (there are benches here). Descend to the left (handrail) in front of the statue. Descend several flights of stone steps to reach the road in front of the church, the Apollinariskirche. Do visit the church as the frescoes and other wall paintings are superb; it is normally left open for visitors.

On leaving the church descend past the Stations of the Cross, admiring the view of the Rhine and the town of Remagen. Continue ahead to an underpass on the left. Those in need of accommodation or refreshment should take this underpass to enter Remagen. Otherwise turn left at the road opposite and follow the route description given in Stage 3.

STAGE 3
Remagen to Bad Breisig: 15.1km (9.4 miles)

LOCATIONS	DISTANCES			
	Sectional		Accumulative	
	kms	miles	kms	miles
REMAGEN (55m; 180ft)	-	-	35.3	21.9
Bad Bodendorf	4.2	2.6	39.5	24.5
SINZIG (73m; 239ft)	3.5	2.2	43.0	26.7
BAD BREISIG (77m; 252ft)	7.4	4.6	50.4	31.3

FACILITIES

Hotels, pensions and B&B establishments in private houses will be found in both Sinzig, at the half-way stage of the walk, and at Bad Breisig. The tourist office in the latter town is in Albert Mertes Strasse.

There are campsites at Kripp, opposite Linz am Rhein, and at journey's end at Bad Breisig. Both are situated on the banks of the Rhine (the Bad Breisig campsite is a little to the north of the town centre). Another campsite lies beneath the fortress of Burg Rheineck, a few kilometres south-east of Bad Breisig, passed en route on the RHW (see Stage 4). There is also a campsite on the right bank at Bad Honningen, opposite Bad Breisig.

Youth hostellers will have problems until they reach Koblenz (see Stage 5).

Shops (including supermarkets), restaurants, cafés and banks will be found in both Sinzig and Bad Breisig.

The village of Bad Bodendorf, passed through on the RHW between Sinzig and Bad Breisig, has shops, including a small supermarket, cafés, a snack bar and a bank, as well as a guesthouse (Gasthof Cholin).

MAPS

1:50,000: Naturpark. Rhein-Westerwald (Landesvermessungsamt Rheinland-Pfalz).

1:25,000: Naturpark Rhein-Westerwald, Blatt 1 - West (Landesvermessungsamt Rheinland-Pfalz).

PLACES OF INTEREST

Ahr valley

The RHW crosses the Ahr valley at Bad Bodendorf, half-way between Remagen and Sinzig. The River Ahr is one of the principal tributaries of the Rhine; it flows into the Rhine at Bad Kripp, south of Remagen, but has it source over 80km (50 miles) away in the Eifel range of hills, which border with the Belgian Ardennes. If time is available the walker is thoroughly recommended to spend some time exploring the Ahr valley further, for it is one of the most attractive regions of this part of Germany, with many ruined castles, forests and vineyards. Head up the valley to Bad Neuenahr-Ahrweiler where there is a youth hostel (see Appendix A), and on to the Upper Ahrtal, where Altenahr is especially picturesque. Alas, several days will be required to do this beautiful region full justice. The valley is famous for its Burgundies and other red wines. There is a long distance path along the valley, known as the Rotweinwanderweg (Red Wine Path).

Sinzig

Like so many of the Rhineland towns, Sinzig is Roman in origin, known in former times as Sentiacum. It is a small town, strategically and safely situated on the southern slopes above the Ahr valley, near the confluence of the River Ahr with the Rhine. Its main feature of note is the quite stunning, albeit fairly small, thirteenth century Church of St Peter. The Romanesque church, dedicated in 1241, is conspicuous because of its yellow and white exterior walls. Inside will be found a rather interesting skeleton, known as Vogt von Sinzig, of uncertain date, which was found in the neighbouring fields. Nearby is the attractive Zehnthof (Tithe House) which can also be visited. The town castle dates from the fourteenth century, but today houses the local history museum, built in the nineteenth.

Linz am Rhein and Burg Ockenfels

On the right bank, opposite Kripp, stands the pretty old town of Linz, crammed with beautifully restored, half-timbered houses. Its twin town gates, known as the Rheintor and the Neutor (Rhine Gate and New Gate) are all that remain of the old town wall fortifications, which were destroyed in 1861. Prior to this period the town was of considerable importance, being the summer residence of the Archbishop of Cologne. Buildings of note include the Romanesque Church of St Martin, the town castle and the Town Hall, situated in the centre of the town. To the north of Linz am Rhein lies another Romantic Rhineland castle, Burg Ockenfels. Medieval in origin, the fortress was destroyed and lay in ruins for several centuries, until it was restored, later than most, in the period between the two World Wars. It is now a hotel, from whose rooms there are excellent views of the Ahr and Rhine valleys.

Bad Breisig
This popular holiday resort on the left bank, the endpoint of this stage, is, as the name suggests, a spa. The town has three thermal springs, pleasant public gardens and several attractive seventeenth and eighteenth century houses.

Bad Honningen
Bad Honningen is another spa town, situated on the right bank opposite Bad Breisig. Although the settlement dates back to Roman times, the town really only grew to importance after 1813, when a source of carbon dioxide was discovered issuing from the ground. The carbonated spring, the Dreikönigsquelle, is the source of the carbonated water for which the town is known: Bad Honningen has the distinction of being the greatest producer of carbonic acid in Germany. Overlooking the northern end of the town is Schloss Arenfels, originally built as a fortress in 1260, but completely renovated in 1849 by the architect who was responsible for the Dom at Cologne. Schloss Arenfels is a typical Romantic Rhineland castle, but is unusual for having the same number of windows and of steps as there are days in the year: 365.

SUMMARY
Not a long section today, under 10 miles in length, followed by a walk of equal length tomorrow. Keen long distance walkers could even consider combining Stages 3 and 4 into one long day section, although this would leave even fast walkers with little time to explore the towns and villages passed en route.

Although a relatively short stage there are several climbs and descents, as the route keeps to relatively high ground well to the west of the Rhine, not returning to the shore of the great river until the end of the stage at Bad Breisig. The RHW crosses the Ahr valley, a major tributary of the Rhine, between Bad Bodendorf and Sinzig. The railway that runs along the Ahr valley is crossed at Bad Bodendorf, just a few metres from the village's railway station, so that a further exploration of the valley and the Eifel range of hills that lie to the east could easily be made from here.

The Trail offers a mixture of woodland walking, on generally good tracks and footpaths, with ambles through a number of attractive towns and villages where there are opportunities for obtaining

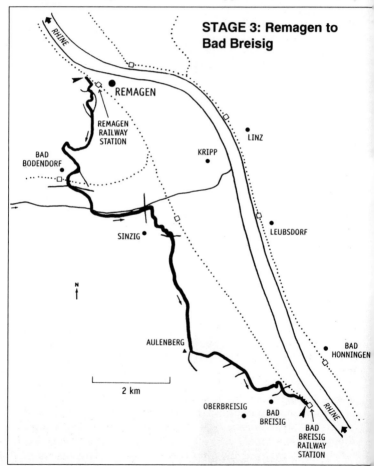

Deutsches Eck, Koblenz (Stages 5 & 6)
The extensively wooded, deep valley of Mühltal (Stage 6)

St Goarshausen, on the right bank of the River Rhine (Stages 7 & 8)
A boat passing at Oberwesel (Stage 8)

refreshments. Day's end is spent at the attractive spa town of Bad Breisig, opposite yet another Rhine Spa, Bad Honningen, so that there is ample opportunity to "take the waters" if the body and mind are beginning to show any signs of fatigue!

THE ROUTE

Return to the underpass which you left yesterday when you walked into the centre of Remagen. Turn onto the road opposite the underpass, but after 50 metres turn left onto the "no through road" (Viktoriabergweg) going uphill (bearing 225 degrees magnetic). Climb steeply, bear sharply to the left at a house to continue the climb. Climb a flight of steps to cross a road and continue ahead still ascending, now on a poorly surfaced track. The track passes some houses to enter a field: continue ahead uphill, still heading south, soon bearing right to enter woodland. Opposite a garden on your right be sure to turn left (bearing 110 degrees magnetic) on another "R" waymarked footpath. This leads to a narrow, poorly surfaced lane: cross it to follow the footpath ahead. The footpath leads to another road: cross it to follow the track ahead, signposted "Wanderweg nach Bodendorf". After about 80 metres bear left on the "R" waymarked footpath. The trail passes an underground reservoir and several boards displaying the geology and natural history of the area.

Keep ahead at a track junction and ahead again at another one, where red, green and blue waymarked local trails head off to both left and right. The path descends steeply. After about 80 metres a crossing track is reached: turn right here, heading west (local route No. 5 continues ahead, downhill at this point). Later ignore a track to the left, but remain on the main track as it bends to the right. The track emerges at a surfaced lane on a hairpin bend. Continue ahead, downhill on the lane, following local route No. 6. Follow this narrow country lane downhill between fields to reach a T-junction on the outskirts of Bodendorf: take the surfaced path downhill, to meet a second road, where you bear slightly left to follow a path to a third road, where you turn right.

Follow this road (Schützenstrasse) to a T-junction in the centre of the village. Turn right here to walk past the attractive houses of the village. Bear left along Bahnhofstrasse to cross the railway line. Cross the main road ahead at the traffic lights to walk down Bäderstrasse (NB: there is a good *schnell imbiss* (snack bar) on the right here). Take

65

Houses in the main street at Bad Bodendorf

the first left turn (Schillerstrasse). Bear right at the end of this road on a metalled footpath between fields. Turn right at a T-junction to pass a solitary stone tower and war cemetery on your right. Cross a stream via a footbridge and bear left at the far side of a lake to follow a footpath on the left bank of a river, passing an aviary and small animal park.

On reaching a footbridge by power cables, turn right to cross over the bridge and then left to follow the right bank of the river downstream. Keep to the riverbank. About 300 metres after passing under a roadbridge turn right away from the river onto a large car parking area, heading for the church whose steeple is seen ahead. Follow the road as it bends to right and left to reach a crossroads by a pedestrian crossing. Turn left on this road for about 100 metres before turning right onto a footpath which heads for the church. Follow the footpath to the left of this large building to reach a main road. Turn left along this road for about 200 metres to reach a stone statue on the right-hand side of the road. The statue is of Friedrich I Barbarossa.

Climb the steps 50 metres to the east of this statue, passing the war memorial. Pass to the right of the church, in the central square of

Sinzig, to turn left down Zehnthofstrasse. After this road swings sharply to the right, turn left on a waymarked footpath and follow this to a road by a pedestrian crossing and a fragment of the old town wall. Head south along Essigkrug, located 40 metres to the east of this wall. Cross another road to keep ahead on the "no through road" signposted to Assessorenweg and Vogelsangstrasse, but after 60 metres take the right fork, Helenenbergstrasse. Where this ends take the poorly surfaced track to the right of a house. Climb on this track to a trail T-junction where you turn left to continue the ascent, heading towards the south. Climb the hill to pass to the right of a wooden shelter, after which there is a small shrine.

At the top of the hill continue ahead on the main track, heading south-south-east and later south across the high level plateau. Follow the "R" waymarks at any track junctions encountered, maintaining a southerly direction. About 2km after the ascent, it is important to locate a "R" waymarked left turn onto a track heading east (100 degrees magnetic). Swing to the left with the main track on reaching a cross-tracks and later continue ahead (east-north-east, 65 degrees magnetic) at a multi cross-tracks by a "Wasser-Schutzgebiet" signpost, but only for 40 metres: then take the "R" waymarked track on the right (south-east, 130 degrees magnetic). Maintain direction at several crossing tracks, following the "R" waymarks. The waymarking is fortunately quite clear in this area.

Eventually a point is reached where local route No. 4, which has been coincident with the "R" trail for some distance, turns to the left (east), whereas you follow the "R" waymarks uphill to the south to reach a small wooden shelter, a couple of benches and a viewpoint. Turn left (south-east) here on a footpath which follows the top of the escarpment. The path eventually begins a zigzagging descent towards the Rhine valley. On reaching a track T-junction turn right for 100 metres before turning left steeply downhill on a zigzagging footpath, which emerges on a road on the outskirts of Bad Breisig. Turn right to walk along this road.

Where this main road swings sharply to the right continue ahead along Backesgasse. Bear left with the road and then right to walk alongside the railway lines. (If the railway station is required then continue ahead to reach it, but to follow the Rheinhöhenweg turn off at the tennis courts). To continue along the RHW turn to the route description in Stage 4.

STAGE 4
Bad Breisig to Andernach: 15.6km (9.7 miles)

LOCATIONS	DISTANCES			
	Sectional		Accumulative	
	kms	miles	kms	miles
BAD BREISIG (77m; 252ft)	-	-	50.4	31.3
Burg Rheineck (161m; 528ft)	2.2	1.4	52.6	32.7
Reuterslei (217m; 711ft)	0.4	0.2	53.0	32.9
Brohl-Lützing (66m; 216ft)	2.1	1.3	51.1	34.2
Alkerhof (223m; 731ft)	1.5	0.9	56.6	35.1
Höhe Buche (318m; 1043ft)	0.9	0.6	57.5	35.7
Knopshof (308m; 1009ft)	0.8	0.5	58.3	36.2
Geishugelhof	0.7	0.4	59.0	36.6
Hochkreuz	3.0	1.9	62.0	38.5
Krahnenberg (182m; 597ft)	3.1	1.9	65.1	40.4
ANDERNACH (67m; 220ft)	0.9	0.6	66.0	41.0

FACILITIES
There are shops, including a supermarket, cafés, and a bank in Brohl-Lützing.

Andernach offers all facilities including banks, supermarkets, restaurants, cafés, and a variety of hotels and B&B style accommodation at all prices. The tourist office in Andernach is on Läufstrasse. Andernach Railway Station, on Kurfürstendamm, is passed en route.

A good campsite (Camping Rheineck) is passed en route, beneath the fortress of Burg Rheineck, a few kilometres south-east of Bad Breisig. There is another campsite at Brohl-Lützing, but note that there is no campsite in the vicinity of Andernach. On the right bank there is a campsite north-west of Leutesdorf.

There are a few hotels, pensions and a restaurant passed on the RHW, or within easy access; these are given in the route description below.

MAPS
1:50,000: Naturpark Rhein-Westerwald (Landesvermessungsamt Rheinland-Pfalz).

1:25,000: Naturpark Rhein-Westerwald, Blatt 1 - West (Landesvermessungsamt Rheinland-Pfalz).

PLACES OF INTEREST

Burg Rheineck

Perched on a 182m (597ft) cliff above the left bank of the Rhine to the
south-east of Bad Breisig, this fortress, originally built in the eleventh
century, has been destroyed and rebuilt several times during its
turbulent history. Owned by the Archbishop-Electors of Cologne for
a considerable period, it was last destroyed in 1689 by the French. The
present building dates from 1832, when it was bought and rebuilt by
the rich Bethmann-Hollweg banking family. Alas, the castle is not
now open to the public.

Brohl

The Brohl is another principal valley system which originates from
the Eifel hills to the west and slowly descends to meet the left bank at
Brohl-Lützing. The quarrying of volcanic pumice was a principal
industry in the area for many centuries, bringing considerable
prosperity to the region. The rock was used, in particular, to build sea
walls, the neighbouring Rhine offering an easy means of transportation
to the Dutch coast.

   South-west of Brohl is the Benedictine Abbey of Maria Laach,
situated in a picturesque setting beside the lake of Laacher See, on the
edge of the Eifel, and worth a detour to visit if time is available.
Founded in 1093 the complex contains a twelfth century Romanesque
six-towered abbey church, which has modern stained glass windows.
The monks are very industrious, operating craft shops for tourists
and singing Gregorian chant.

Leutesdorf

Compared to its neighbours, the village of Leutesdorf is relatively
small. Situated on the right bank, amidst many vineyards, the village
possesses several restored half-timbered houses and a fine baroque
seventeenth century Pilgrim Church of the Holy Cross. North-west
of Leutesdorf, on the island of Hammersteiner Werth in the middle
of the Rhine, is the eleventh century Hammerstein Castle.

Andernach

Andernach, part industrial and part holiday resort, is a large, pleasant

Part of the old town walls of Andernach

town built on the site of the Roman fort known as Autunnacum, well worth a few hours' exploration. It is one of the oldest settlements on the Rhine, having celebrated its 2000 year anniversary in 1988. Not only did the Romans appreciate its strategic situation, but it was later a Royal Court in Charlemagne's time, before passing into the hands of the Archbishop-Electors of Cologne - Andernach was the southern limit of their territory. Legend surrounds the history of the town, as it does with so many Rhineland locations. The most enchanting story is that of the Ardernachern Bäckerjungen (Andernach's Baker Boys), who saved the town from destruction by repulsing an invading army from nearby Linz by setting loose a swarm of bees which routed the attacking force; the story is portrayed in stone in the sculptures to be found on the Rhine Gate (Rheintor) at the northern end of the town.

Much of the Old Town or Altstadt dates from the medieval

period. The town ramparts are thirteenth century, built over earlier Roman ones, and in very good condition, not having been slighted, as so many were in the seventeenth and eighteenth centuries in the Rhineland. There are several fortified gateways, the most notable of which is the picturesque fifteenth century Round Tower (Runder Turm), dating from 1448 and overlooking the Rhine. Much of the town castle also remains, despite being damaged by the French in 1688.

There are two churches of note in the town: the twin-towered thirteenth century Pfarrkirche Maria Himmelfahrt (Church of Our Lady) is late Romanesque; Christuskirche is Gothic and a former monastery. The sixteenth century Town Hall (Altes Rathaus) is another notable building in the centre of the town. The local museum is housed in the Renaissance mansion house known as the Haus von der Leyen.

One of the unique features of the town, and a prominent landmark, is the old wooden sixteenth century Rhine Crane, which is a reminder of the town's rich industrial history. It was in daily working use until just before the First World War, and is still in working order.

Several festivals are held in the town, the most well known being the Summer Carnival and the Thousand Lights (Die Tausende Lichten) held in the first week in September, a festival of fireworks and illuminations.

SUMMARY

More undulating country today as the trail lives up to its "High Route" designation. Rhineland castles are beginning to become more frequent, although they are not yet as thick on the ground as they will be in a few days' time, south of Koblenz. Burg Rheineck is passed en route, soon after leaving Bad Breisig. Another major valley system is crossed today, at Brohl, the river of which also rises in the Eifel hills to the west, and meets the Rhine at Brohl-Lützing. Further climbing leads over the Höhe Buche which, at 318m, a little over 1000ft above sea level, is the highest point reached on the walk so far. Woodland walking again predominates today, but there are nevertheless plenty of places where good views of the Rhine and the surrounding countryside may be had. The last section to Andernach is across open country. Again the day is not over long so there should be plenty of time to enjoy the area and visit the several places of interest.

The stage ends at Andernach, one of the principal towns on this section of the Rhine, where ample accommodation is available and where there is much to see.

THE ROUTE

Return to the tennis courts referred to at the end of Stage 3. At the near side (west side) of the tennis courts turn right off the road (tennis courts now to your left) to take the upper of the two paths behind the courts. Climb on this path to reach a track T-junction where you turn left. Follow this track to a path junction where you also turn left (at a signpost to "Kapelle 20 min & Camping"), following the "R" waymarks. This delightful path leads to the deep and wooded Rheineck valley.

Descend to the road. Those in need of hotel or

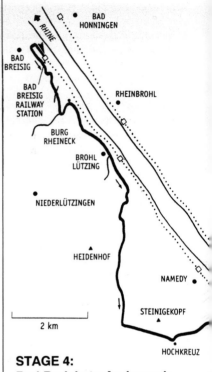

**STAGE 4:
Bad Breisig to Andernach**

pension accommodation should turn left here (hotels and *zimmer frei* will be found within a couple of hundred metres). Otherwise cross the road to bear left with the stream along Mühlenstrasse. This leads, in about 400 metres, to a campsite (Camping Rheineck). Take the footpath on the left immediately in front of the campsite entrance. This is signposted as "Viehweg zur Burg Rheineck und Reuterslay". The path climbs steeply to reach an old stone seat above which there is a black cross mounted on a pedestal. Turn right here following the "R" waymarks uphill. Turn left at a path T-junction to walk along the edge of the escarpment above the Rhine. This leads to a panoramic viewpoint above the Rhine, opposite Bad Honningen/Rheinbrohl.

Descend from the viewpoint, steeply at first, and continue to follow this well-engineered path along the hillside. The path descends to a road; keep straight ahead descending the steep road to reach a crossroads. Cross over to follow Bergstrasse ahead. A hundred metres after the church at Brohl-Lützing bear left to descend to a T-junction. Here turn right to walk through the village (shops and cafés, a supermarket and a bank). Turn right at the junction in front of the post office and 50 metres later turn left onto a track at an E 8 signpost (Nordsee-Rhein-Donau) and another indicating Andernach 3 hours. Thirty metres after crossing a railway line turn right onto a narrow footpath (another signpost indicating Andernach here). Climb on this path to reach a circular wooden shelter and splendid viewpoint of Brohl-Lützing and the Rhine.

Continue along the path, climbing to a bench and another viewpoint of the Rhine. The path leads to a very steep set of steps hewn into the rock: climb these (handrail provided) to reach a flagpole. Continue the climb on the path to reach yet another viewpoint

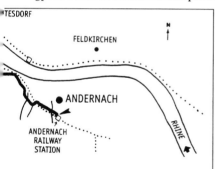

and seat. The path levels at this point. Continue to a track T-junction to the right of large farm buildings. Turn right on the track, but a few metres before entering the wood bear left on a footpath to enter the trees and walk ahead at a cross-track. The trail climbs in a woodland gully to reach a crossing track: turn right here. The Rheinhöhenweg is now crossing the Höhe Buche at 318m (a little over 1000ft above sea level), the highest point reached on the trail so far. Walk ahead at the next cross-tracks, and ahead again where a trail joins from the left, to reach a signpost which indicates 2 hours to Andernach.

Continue ahead on the forest track to a track T-junction near to a cottage: turn left here and ignore the "T" waymarked track on the right reached within 40 metres. Pass the cottage of Knopshof and head southwards, now over open country. Keep ahead at the large Geishugelhof farm complex. Continue to a crossroads which stands between two large pylons carrying HT cable. Turn left (east) here. After about 600 metres this track runs alongside woodland. Later ignore a track on the left which descends into the forest, but instead keep ahead on the main track beside the wood, to pass a large stone cross (Hochkreuz) and two stone seats, which are on the right of the track. Bear left at this point to reach a sign indicating "Haltet den Wald Sauber". Locate a track a few metres to the right (east) of this notice. Follow this track north-eastwards through the wood, after 100 metres taking the right fork (east) downhill. Keep ahead at a cross-tracks by a wooden shelter. Namedy, Leutesdorf and the Rhine soon come into view below left.

The trail eventually passes to the left of a large restaurant, from where a wide view of the Rhine opens out. Bear to the right at the viewing platform just below the restaurant. Descend to reach a large main road. At the road turn sharply to the left to walk through an underpass, so reaching the outskirts of Andernach. Continue the descent ahead to reach a road T-junction where you turn left downhill. Turn right at the traffic lights onto Breite Strasse, in front of the railway lines. Turn left at the next set of traffic lights onto Bahnhofstrasse and then right along Kurfürstendamm, signposted to the Bahnhof. Turn right in front of Andernach railway station and then left along the main road, Breite Strasse.

STAGE 5
Andernach to Koblenz: 26.4km (16.4 miles)

LOCATIONS	DISTANCES			
	Sectional		Accumulative	
	kms	miles	kms	miles
ANDERNACH (67m; 220ft)	-	-	66.0	41.0
Miesenheim (80m; 262ft)	6.5	4.0	72.5	45.0
Kettig (76m; 249ft)	3.5	2.2	76.0	47.2
Kärlich	1.8	1.1	77.8	48.3
Mühlheim	1.6	1.0	79.4	49.3
Rübenacher Höhe (195m; 639ft)	2.3	1.4	81.7	50.7
Rübenach	1.3	0.8	83.0	51.5
Güls (70m; 230ft)	5.1	3.2	88.1	54.7
KOBLENZ (Town Centre)	4.3	2.7	92.4	57.4

FACILITIES

Koblenz is a major city and as such has all main facilities. Accommodation is plentiful, from hotels of all categories, to pensions, B&Bs, a youth hostel and campsite. There is a tourist office opposite the main railway station (open 8.30-18.00 Monday to Friday & 11.30-18.00 Saturdays, closed Sundays), and another near the Rhine at Konrad-Adenauer-Ufer.

Koblenz Youth Hostel is one of the finest in Germany, being housed in the giant Festung or fortress on the right bank of the Rhine in Ehrenbreitstein. There is a superb view from the hostel over to the Deutsches Eck and the Mosel. Koblenz campsite (Campingplatz Rhein-Mosel) is in Lützel, at the confluence of the Rhine and Mosel, opposite Deutsches Eck. It is reached from the main town by taking the passenger ferry across the Mosel from Deutsches Eck (circa 60 pfennigs one way). This ferry runs more or less continually, except during the winter months, starting quite early in the morning. A stay in the campsite allows you to savour the fine view of the opposite banks of the Rhine and Mosel.

Those seeking refreshments before reaching the day's end at Koblenz should find sustenance in the town of Kärlich (a café/restaurant is passed en route). Güls, a small town on the left (west) bank of the Mosel, a satellite town of Koblenz, has plenty of shops, cafés and restaurants, B&B accommodation, a bank and a railway station.

There are railway stations at Andernach, Weissenthurm (off-route) Urmitz-Bahnhof (off-route), Güls (slightly off-route), and at Koblenz. Koblenz has two railway stations, one to the north of the Mosel and one to its south - the latter is the main station or *Hauptbahnhof*. The main bus station is adjacent to the *Hauptbahnhof*.

MAPS

1:50,000: Naturpark Rhein-Westerwald plus Der Rhein von Bingen bis Koblenz (Landesvermessungsamt Rheinland-Pfalz). Note that by using these two maps there is a "gap" of approximately 5km (3.1 miles) in the RHW, between Kärlich and Rübenach, not covered by either map.

1:25,000: Naturpark Rhein-Westerwald, Blatt 1 - West, plus Naturpark Rhein-Westerwald, Blatt 3 - Süd, plus Koblenz und Umgebung (all Landesvermessungsamt Rheinland-Pfalz).

PLACES OF INTEREST

Neuwied

The Rhine narrows at the Andernach Gap, but further to the south-east widens again at an area known as the Neuwied Basin, in which there is an island, the Weissenthurmer Werth. This region was the site of the first recorded bridge over the Rhine, a Roman construction, which carried Julius Caesar's armies when they crossed the Rhine in 55 BC. Nothing remains of this bridge today, but a modern bridge, the Raiffeisen Brücke, links Weissenthurm, the sister town of Andernach, on the left bank with the large town of Neuwied (New Palace) on the right bank. The town dates from the mid-seventeenth century. The palace is situated near the town and was built in the first half of the eighteenth century, its design based on that of Versailles. There are a number of interesting eighteenth century buildings in the town, and also of note are the remains of the twelfth century Altenwied Castle. There are also a number of attractive old half-timbered buildings in nearby Engers, to the east of Neuwied.

Koblenz

Koblenz is one of the principal cities on the German Rhine (population about 115,000), the third largest visited on the Rheinhöhenweg, after Bonn and Mainz. There has been a settlement here for about 2000 years, the Romans being the first to grasp the military and commercial significance of the area, the meeting point of two of the mightiest rivers of Western Europe. The Roman town, built in AD 14, was originally called Confluentes, ie. the settlement at the confluence of the Rhine and the Mosel (Moselle). Whoever controlled this point could therefore control access to both of these major waterways. The region has considerable symbolic significance for the German race, in particular the point at which the Mosel flows into the Rhine, the Deutsches Eck (German Corner). This was the first acquisition of the German Order of Knights in 1216, and so was of considerable military significance. In 1897 a giant equestrian statue of Kaiser Wilhelm I was erected at the Deutsches Eck. It was destroyed during the Second World War, but has now been rebuilt as the huge Unity Monument. The base of the monument itself is huge, consisting of several flights of high stone steps. On reaching the Deutsches Eck on the RHW the first section of the trail, from Bonn to Koblenz, has been completed, so this prominent landmark is also significant for the Rhine walker. Climb the steps at the Deutsches Eck to reach a point immediately below the huge statue - from here there is a good view of the confluence of the Mosel and Rhine. The Deutsches Eck and the Burg are floodlit at night. The whole scene is perhaps seen best from the campsite on the far bank.

From the Deutsches Eck the enormous fortress, clearly visible on the opposite (right) bank, is the Ehrenbreitstein Festung. Originally built in the tenth century the fortress passed to Archbishop Poppo in 1020, the ruler of Koblenz at the time, and remained in the hands of the Archbishop-Electors of Trier for several centuries, until it was finally successfully sieged by the French at the end of the eighteenth century. After the defeat of Napoleon the Prussians restored the damaged fortress after 1816. Today it is the home of one of the best youth hostels in Germany, as well as the Landesmuseum. The Festung, perched on a hill above the right bank of the Rhine, can be reached either by chairlift or on foot. There is a superb view of Deutsches Eck and the two rivers from the terraces here.

The Rhein Promenade, which runs all alongside the river through Koblenz, starts at the Deutsches Eck, and the RHW commences its long journey south from the city by sampling a section of the Promenade. The Weindorf (Wine Village) is situated along this promenade near Pfaffendorfer Bridge. Built originally for a wine exhibition in 1926, the Weindorf is the place to go for entertainment and to sample a large selection of Rhine wines.

There are many fine buildings to visit and admire in this attractive city. There are three principal churches of interest, all built on Roman foundations and all much restored since the 1950s:

1. St Kastor's Church. This twin-towered church in the heart of the Old Town is Romanesque in style and dates from the ninth to the twelfth centuries.
2. Liebfrauenkirche. Twelfth-fifteenth century, a mixture of Romanesque and Gothic styles.
3. St Florin's Church, an eleventh-fourteenth century Romanesque-Gothic Protestant church, located in the Florinsmarkt.

Other buildings of interest include:

1. The Castle, the Alte Burg, was originally fortified, then converted to a Renaissance Palace; it now houses the City Library.
2. The Rathaus or Town Hall, which is Baroque in style and dates from 1700.
3. Altes Kaufhaus - this houses the Mittelrhein Museum (paintings and sculptures).
4. The Electoral Palace on the Rhine. This was built by Clemens Wenceslas, the last Archbishop-Elector of Trier, and finished in 1786.

A visit to Koblenz is particularly rewarding in August, when the annual Rhine in Flames Festival (Der Rhein in Flammen) features a spectacular fireworks display.

Finally Koblenz is of historical importance to the traveller and tourist. It was here in 1823 that Karl Baedeker began publishing his famous series of travel guidebooks, including, of course, one to the Rhineland.

The Mosel Valley

The River Mosel (Moselle in French) rises in the Vosges range of hills in north-eastern France, later forming the frontier between Germany and Luxembourg, finally flowing north-eastwards through Germany between the Eifel range of hills to the north and the Hunsrück to the south, to enter the Rhine at the Deutsches Eck in Koblenz. The Mosel valley, like that of the Rhine, is world famous as a wine-producing

A Romanesque-Gothic church in Florinsmarkt, Koblenz

area, mile after mile of its south-facing slopes being covered in vineyards. Those with time available can either sample the Mosel valley on foot (recommended - see below) or take a few days off from the RHW to visit some of the attractive and interesting towns along the valley (frequent express and local trains, and also several bus services). The principal road along the valley, popular with tourists, is the Mosel Weinstrasse (Wine Road).

The main places of interest from Koblenz to Trier are described briefly below. For more detail a general travel guide is useful - see Appendix C.

Winningen
A town with many attractive half-timbered houses and home of the oldest wine festival in Germany.

Kobern-Gondorf
Really two towns, strung out along the Mosel. Kobern boasts the oldest half-timbered house in the Rhineland-Palatinate, dating from 1321. See also the Upper and Lower castles (Oberburg and Niederburg).

Burg Eltz
This is a must for any visitor to the Mosel valley as it contains one of the two intact medieval castles in the Rhineland-Palatinate (the other is the Marksburg, above the Rhine - see Stage 6). The castle has been the home of the Eltz family for thirty generations. There are guided tours.

Karden
Old half-timbered houses, the Romanesque/Gothic Church of St Kastor and two castles (the Wildburg and Burg Treis) are the main items of interest.

Cochem
One of the principal towns on the Mosel, often packed with tourists. The main attraction is the town castle, the Reichsburg (the original castle was destroyed in 1689). See also the baroque *Rathaus* (Town Hall) and St Martin's Church.

Beilstein
Small town which also boasts a castle, Burg Beilstein.

Alf
The tenth century Burg Arras towers above this village, offering panoramic views of the Mosel valley.

Traben-Trarbach
Like Kobern-Gondorf further east, Traben-Trarbach is a double town, Traben on the north bank of the Mosel and Trarbach on the south bank. Traben contains the ruins of two castles, Schloss Grevenburg and Mount Royal, whilst Trarbach has some attractive half-timbered houses and nineteenth century villas.

Bernkastel-Kues
Another double town, also popular with tourists. The area abounds with vineyards. The ruins of the thirteenth century Burg Landshut and the Renaissance *Rathaus* (Town Hall) are the main things to see.

Neumagen-Dhron
The claim to fame of this town is that it is the oldest wine-producing town in Germany, its origins being Roman. The Roman remains, the Heimatmuseum and the Peterskapelle are all worth a visit.

Trier
If you only have time to visit one place on the German Mosel, then let it be Trier. Trier is the oldest city in Germany, founded by the Romans. There is an abundance of accommodation of all kinds, including a youth hostel. Plan to spend at least a day here. The Roman monuments are the principal attraction, particularly the Porta Nigra (Black Gate), the largest and best preserved city gate of the Classical period in the world, which is perhaps seen to best effect at night when it is illuminated. The eleventh century Romanesque cathedral and the adjacent Gothic Liebfrauenkirche should also be on your itinerary.

MOSELHÖHENWEG

Those with plenty of time to spare and wishing to enjoy more walking in Germany could decide to combine the Rheinhöhenweg with the other major riparian pathway in the region, the Moselhöhenweg. The sister route of the RHW, this follows a "high level" undulating trail on either shore of the Mosel between Koblenz and Trier and beyond. The character of the Moselhöhenweg is similar to that of the Rheinhöhenweg, although the hills surrounding the Mosel, often carpeted in vineyards, are perhaps generally less steep than those above the Rhine. Another difference between the two trails is that the Moselhöhenweg takes paths away from the riverside more often than does the Rheinhöhenweg. This is largely a consequence of the nature of the two rivers: the Mosel follows a far more meandering course than the Rhine, the inland detours of the Moselhöhenweg often cutting off some of the more tightly cut meanders.

There are trails on both the south or right-hand bank of the Mosel (the Hunsrück side of the river) and along the north or left-hand bank (the Eifel side of the river). It is possible to abandon the RHW at Koblenz to follow the Mosel instead, ending your walk at Trier, which has a railway station convenient for the train homewards. Fit and keen walkers, with plenty of holiday available, could leave Koblenz on one of the Moselhöhenweg trails (either the left or right-hand banks) to Trier, or even to Palzem or Wasserbillig, and return to Koblenz on the other Moselhöhenweg trail, to resume the Rheinhöhenweg south to Mainz and Alsheim. Alternatively, the Moselhöhenweg could form the basis of a second, completely separate walking holiday.

If you wish simply to take a day or two off from the Rheinhöhenweg to sample the walking in the Mosel valley along the Moselhöhenweg, the 1:50,000 map "Der Rhein von Bingen bis Koblenz", used for the RHW, covers the Moselhöhenweg on either bank of the river for two or more days from Koblenz, so that it will not be necessary to purchase another map (see below for details of the maps required for the whole of the Moselhöhenweg). The return to Koblenz to resume the RHW would also be easy, either opting to walk back along one of the two Moselhöhenwegs, or taking public transport.

Those with a reading knowledge of German would be able to use the guide booklet entitled simply "Moselhöhenweg", published by Rheinland-Pfalz and available, usually free of charge, by sending an International Reply Coupon to Fremdenverkehrs und Heilbäderverband Rheinland-Pfalz (see Appendix D). However by using the maps, which have the route of the Moselhöhenweg clearly overlaid, you should have few problems of navigation, particularly as the routes are clearly marked on the ground with "M" waymarks, in a similar manner to the "R" waymarking of the RHW.

The maps required for the Moselhöhenweg are as follows:

The whole route is covered by four maps, one at a scale of 1:50,000 and the others at 1:25,000 scale:

Map 1:   Die Mosel von Bernkastel-Kues bis Koblenz (1:50,000)
Map 2:   Bernkastel-Kues/Mosel (1:25,000)
Map 3:   Der Meulenwald und die Mosel bei Schweich (1:25,000)
Map 4:   Trier und Trier-Land (1:25,000)

All of these maps are published by Landesvermessungsamt Rheinland-Pfalz.

Those with the 1:50,000 scale map "Der Rhein von Bingen bis Koblenz" have sufficient map to follow the Moselhöhenweg from Koblenz to Lasserg along the northern route of the Moselhöhenweg and from Koblenz to Eveshausen on the southern route (see below). Those not in possession of a guide to the Moselhöhenweg routes should find the following information useful:

Moselhöhenweg - Southern Route (right-hand bank or Hunsrück side of the River Mosel). Distance: 224km (139 miles). Koblenz to Palzem, via Trier.

The outline of the trail is as follows:
Koblenz > Waldesch > Nassheck > Alken > Brodenbach > Oppenhauser > Beulich > Eveshausen > Lütz > Treis > Bruttig-Fankel > Beilstein > Merl > Zell > Enkirch > Starenburg > Traben-Trarbach > Graach > Bernkastel-kues > Monzelfeld > Horath > Papiermühle > Riol > Fastrau > Ruwer > Trier > Konz > Nittel > Wincheringen > Palzem.

Moselhöhenweg - Northern Route (left-hand bank or Eifel side of the River Mosel). Distance: 164km (102 miles). Koblenz to Wasserbillig (just over the border in Luxembourg), via Trier.

The outline of the trail is as follows:
Koblenz > Wolken > Kobern-Gondorf > Dreckenach > Moselsürsch > Mörz > Münstermaifeld > Metternich > Lasserg > Burg Eltz > Karden > Pommern > Klotten > Cochem > Bremm > St Aldegund > Alf > Reil > Kröv > Kinheim > Urzig > Lieser > Monzel > Piesport > Klüsserath > Ensch > Schweich > Trier > Herresthal > Igel > Wasserbillig.

There is adequate accommodation of all types available on both routes of the Moselhöhenweg.

SUMMARY

Today's stage is the longest section on the trail so far, however the terrain is fairly gentle for the most part. The Rhine heads eastwards after Andernach for several miles before turning fairly sharply to the south to enter Koblenz. The area is fairly built up, with major road and rail communications and an industrial area, Kesselheim and Neuendorf, to the north of Koblenz. However, the RHW avoids all of this by departing from the river for most of the day, heading generally in a south-easterly direction in a more or less direct line for Koblenz.

The walking out of Andernach is practically on the level, but then the trail undulates more as it crosses gentle hills over fields, to visit a number of small towns including Kettig, Kärlich and Mühlheim, these communities all situated well to the south of the Rhine. A climb over Rübenacher Höhe leads to Rübenach village, after which Koblenz begins to beckon, but is not reached before the trail passes through the centre of the pleasant village of Güls, situated

on the west bank of another of Germany's great rivers, the Mosel. Once the Mosel valley is reached there is a great temptation to explore this further, maybe on foot by following part of the Moselhöhenweg (see "Places of Interest" above).

The Mosel is crossed to enter the outskirts of Koblenz. The day finishes with a walk through the city to its mighty cathedral in the centre, and then on to the banks of the Rhine at the famous Deutsches Eck. This town walk is by no means unpleasant but there is the option of avoiding this urban stretch by taking one of the numerous city buses to the city centre. Walkers wanting the Koblenz campsite can reach it by an inexpensive passenger ferry over the Rhine from the Deutsches Eck.

Koblenz is one of the major staging posts on the Rheinhöhenweg, reached after five days of walking from Bonn. By now most walkers will be looking for a day-off from the trail, and this is most certainly the place to do just that. There is such a great deal to see that justice cannot be given to the city without allocating at least one full day to explore it. Koblenz is a very pleasant, clean and attractive Rhineland city, with several good restaurants and hotels, so a day here would be a relaxing interlude.

THE ROUTE
From the main road, Breite Strasse, near Andernach Railway Station, head east-south-east (115 degrees magnetic) to reach a road junction

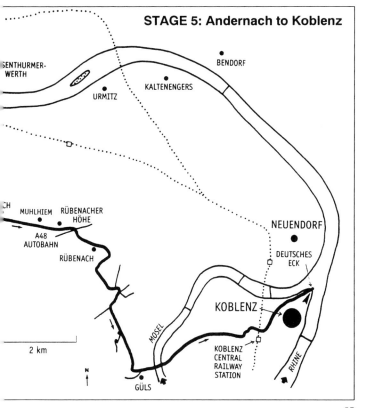

STAGE 5: Andernach to Koblenz

at traffic lights near an old, large, high stone tower. Maintain direction along Schillerring and then Stadionstrasse to pass under the railway line. Eighty metres after passing under this line ignore the road off to the left, but continue ahead. This lane crosses fields, eventually bearing right to take an underpass below the main road. Remain on the road to pass under HT cables and cross a road. Continue ahead (south-east) on a track across the fields. Turn right at a track T-junction for 50 metres and then left on a track that leads to a bridge over a river. Immediately after crossing the bridge turn right on a track on the right (south) bank. Pass under power cables and then under a major road, the track then bending to the left, to follow the line of this road for 300 metres. Fifty metres after the large pylon carrying HT cables, turn right onto another track which passes under the power lines and heads southwards.

Remain on this track to reach a track T-junction, with Nettlehammar farm to the right. Here turn left onto a track which within 200 metres bends to the right by a bench. Remain on this track to pass under three sets of power cables. Continue to a track T-junction where turn right (south-west). Pass a wooden shelter and then follow the course of the River Nettle. Continue to reach a main road at a bridge over the river. Turn left, not on the main road, but along a minor lane a few metres before the main road. Pass an interesting series of track-side "stations of the cross" and pass under another set of power cables. Pass to the left of a small chapel in the middle of the fields and continue on the track, climbing the gentle hills ahead. Be sure to look back at the expansive view to Andernach. At the top of the climb continue straight ahead at a cross-tracks. Continue ahead at the next cross-tracks to pass beneath another set of HT cables after which begin the descent into Kettig.

Keep ahead along Bergastrasse to turn right onto Am Grabengässchen. Cross the road ahead to walk on the footpath to the right of house No. 49. Turn left at the end of the footpath and then right within 80 metres up Holzstrasse. Continue ahead up the hill, passing to the left of a semicircular picnic table and seat. Ignore Kolpingtrasse on the left, but 60 metres afterwards turn left onto a drive, bearing left onto a path after only 10 metres. The trail leads to a track where you turn right, heading east. Keep ahead at the next cross-tracks to reach the outskirts of Kärlich.

Continue ahead along Blütenstrasse for about 120 metres to turn right onto a surfaced drive (E 8 and "R" waymark). Climb to a track junction where you turn left (east) to walk between an orchard on your left and a wooded bank on your right. Continue ahead at the next three cross-tracks, remaining on the track which is surfaced with regular geometrical patterns. Those using the 1:50,000 maps should note that this is the point at which the RHW runs off the sheet entitled "Naturpark Rhein-Westerwald". The route does not run onto the next map in the sequence, entitled "Der Rhein von Bingen bis Koblenz", for about another 5km, but by following the route description below, and the frequent waymarking, no difficulties should be experienced.

Turn left on reaching a road at a T-junction, cross over Waldstrasse and walk along Stationsweg, bearing right at its end along Auf dem Nippes. Within 30 metres turn right along Mühlenstrasse. Pass to the right of a cemetery, cross a main road and continue down Mühlenstrasse. Cross over Hoorweiherstrasse, pass to the left of a café/restaurant and cross the road ahead to walk along a path enclosed between fences between two houses (the one on the right is No. 29). The path climbs between orchards. Be sure to take a left turn in these orchards where indicated (the waymarking is fortunately clear) onto a surfaced track. Turn left at a road T-junction for 40 metres and then right onto another surfaced track (regular geometric patterns again). On reaching a cross-track turn right (south-east) to head uphill on a dirt track. Climb to the top of the hill (Rübenacher Höhe, 195m). Descend on the grassy track to reach the A48 Autobahn. Bear left to follow the track which runs beside this motorway for about 500 metres, to locate an underpass. Walk through this to emerge in the village of Rübenach.

Bear right for 20 metres, then left along Schiesserweg. At the road junction at its end walk ahead along Kruppstrasse. Cross Achener Strasse and walk along the narrow surfaced lane opposite. This soon becomes a narrow grassy footpath which crosses a field to reach a suburban road (the route here joins the 1:50,000 map entitled "Der Rhein von Bingen bis Koblenz"). Keep ahead (south-east), cross a road and continue to a track T-junction. Turn right here and continue to another T-junction where you turn left to cross a railway line and then pass under more HT cables. The trail eventually bends to the left to take a footbridge over a main road. A few metres later ignore the track on the left, but instead turn right at a bench, with the large stable complex now to your left. The surfaced trail heads south, following the course of the main road which is over to your right, to reach a T-junction. Turn right here and then, at a crossroads with the main road to your right, turn left (south-east) on a stony track which crosses the fields. The route passes to the west of Heyerberg (181m); where the track becomes surfaced continue ahead, aiming for the huge tower seen on the hillside to the south-east (note that you will visit this tower on Stage 6 tomorrow). The trail begins a descent, passes a number of "stations of the cross" to reach a superb viewpoint above Güls and the Mosel.

Descend past vineyards and bear right when the outskirts of Güls are reached to walk into the centre of the town. Turn left ("R" and "M" waymarks) on reaching a T-junction. Pass under the left-hand of the two railway bridges to walk down to the bank of the Mosel. Take the pedestrian walkway over the bridge to cross the Mosel. Follow the cycle path on the opposite bank of the river ("R" waymark) alongside the railway line and then follow Unterbreitweg and "M" waymarks. Turn left on reaching a T-junction and then right in about 40 metres along Beatusstrasse. Follow the walkway alongside this road for almost 2km until, just after a small playing field and swimming baths on the left, turn left along Lindenstrasse. Turn right at the traffic lights along In der Goldgrube. At the T-junction bear slightly left aiming for the prominent church (single slender spire). Pass to the left of this building to walk under the road and rail bridges.

At the far side of the railway bridge turn right for the railway station, or, if continuing the walk, left along Oberelöhr. Cross the Moselring to reach Koblenz Cathedral to walk through the main shopping streets of the town, Löhrstrasse followed by Münzstrasse. Turn right at Florinsmarkt and then left in front of the twin-steepled church to reach the bank of the River Mosel at Peter-Altmeier-Ufer. Turn right to walk alongside the river to reach Deutsches Eck, the confluence of the Rhine and the Mosel.

STAGE 6
Koblenz to Boppard: 23.5km (14.6 miles)

LOCATIONS	DISTANCES			
	Sectional		Accumulative	
	kms	miles	kms	miles
KOBLENZ (Town Centre)	-	-	92.4	57.4
KOBLENZ (Deutsches Eck)	1.5	0.9	93.9	58.3
Rhein Lache	2.1	1.3	96.0	59.6
Ritterturz (167m; 548ft)	3.0	1.9	99.0	61.5
Point 296m (970ft)	2.0	1.2	101.0	62.7
Kühkopf (382m; 1252ft)	0.8	0.5	101.8	63.2
Schüllerhof (335m; 1098ft)	1.6	1.0	103.4	64.2
Merkurtempel (352m; 1154ft)	0.9	0.6	104.3	64.8
Waldesch (309m; 1013ft)	2.4	1.5	106.7	66.3
Bruder-Tönnes-Hügel (420m; 1377ft)	2.6	1.6	109.3	67.9
Vierseenblick (274m; 898ft)	3.7	2.3	113.0	70.2
Gedeonseck	0.3	0.2	113.3	70.4
BOPPARD (67m; 220ft)	2.6	1.6	115.9	72.0

FACILITIES

Boppard, the end point of today's stage, offers a wide selection of hotels, guesthouses and B&Bs. Youth hostellers will have to wait until they reach St Goar at the end of Stage 7. Boppard Tourist Office is on Karmeliterstrasse. There are shops of most types, including a supermarket and banks.

Those wishing to divide the stage into two shorter sections could make use of the facilities in the Hunsrück village of Waldesch, just over half-way between Koblenz and Boppard. There is a hotel-restaurant and another *gasthof* in Waldesch, as well as a bank and some shops. A welcome break before reaching Boppard can be taken in the café/restaurants of Vierseenblick and Gedeonseck (rooms available) which are passed en route a couple of miles before Boppard. A rest at one of these is recommended for the fine views from their terraces of the Rhine valley below.

There is no camping in Boppard itself, but there is a campsite at Sonneck, some distance north of the town, alongside the left bank of the Rhine.

Those who venture across the Rhine, perhaps to explore Lahnstein and the Lahn valley, will find several hotels and a choice of B&Bs in Lahnstein; there are also two campsites here, Burg Lahneck in the grounds of the castle, and another called Rhein-Lahn-Eck. Those who leave the Rheinhöhenweg to delve further up the Lahn valley will find a youth hostel in Diez.

Regular local train services operate between Koblenz and Boppard, journey time about 15mins. Local bus services are also in operation. On the right shore of the Rhine trains run from Koblenz to Lahnstein, Braubach and beyond.

MAPS

1:50,000: Der Rhein von Bingen bis Koblenz (Landesvermessungsamt Rheinland-Pfalz).

1:25,000: Koblenz und Umgebung plus Naturpark Nassau, Blatt 1 - West (Landesvermessungsamt Rheinland-Pfalz).

PLACES OF INTEREST

Stolzenfels Castle

The massive *Schloss* (Castle) of Stolzenfels stands on a wooded hillside above the left bank of the Rhine, between Koblenz and Rhens. Rheinhöhenweg walkers can reach it by making a detour of about a kilometre from the trail. The castle dates from the thirteenth century (constructed around 1242 by the Archbishop-Elector of Trier) and was built on the site of an earlier Roman fort. However, the medieval fortress was destroyed by the French in 1688/9, but was rebuilt in Gothic style by King Friedrich-Wilhelm IV in the 1830s, when the present battlements were added. The interior is ornate and houses a museum of armour and weaponry. There is a magnificent view from the castle down to the Rhine below, with the city of Koblenz to the north.

Lahnstein

The town of Lahnstein is situated opposite Stolzenfels Castle, on the right bank of the Rhine, at the foot of the Lahn valley, where the River Lahn flows into the Rhine. The most notable thing about the town, which is divided into Lower (Nieder Lahnstein), alongside the Rhine, and Upper (Ober Lahnstein) sections, is the medieval fortress of Burg Lanneck, which dominates the town and from which there is a good view of the Rhine below. Originally built in the thirteenth century, the castle was much restored in the nineteenth. Burg Lahneck marked the start of the region ruled by the Bishops of Mainz; their territory stretched south from here, across the country that you are about to explore over the next few days, to Mainz itself.

The Lahn valley

The Lahn valley is not included in the Rheinhöhenweg, but if a day or more is available when you reach Koblenz, then a detour to visit this attractive valley is highly recommended. The River Lahn flows into the right bank of the Rhine and its valley heads eastwards from the Rhine valley, a little to the south of Koblenz. The town of Lahnstein (see above) lies at the confluence of the two rivers.

The Lahn valley has steeply wooded banks and a succession of charming villages and towns, surrounded by pleasant hillscapes. Heading up the valley from the Rhine the first town of any size encountered is Bad Ems, about a dozen kilometres from Lahnstein. This elegant, expensive spa town, which was fashionable with the nineteenth century aristocracy, including King Wilhelm I of Prussia, was the scene in 1870 of important political events which hastened the onset of the six month Franco-Prussian war and led to the unification of Germany, with the formation of the Second German Reich. Nassau, a few kilometres further east up the Lahn valley, also has historical associations, with the influential Oranien-Nassau European dynasty. Finally, if sufficient time is still available, travel much further up the Lahn valley to Diez, where a stay can be made at the youth hostel which is part of the medieval castle which dominates the area. Guided tours can also be taken around a second castle, the baroque Schloss Oranienstein. Diez is close to Limburg, famous for its cathedral, another German city worth a visit.

Rhens

The Rheinhöhenweg leaves the bank of the Rhine for much of the way between Koblenz and Boppard, preferring an inland route amongst the hills and woods to the west of the river, and consequently it misses the picturesque small town of Rhens, situated on the left bank. Make a detour to visit Rhens if you can, by bus if need be from Koblenz or Boppard. Medieval fortifications surround the many half-timbered houses of the town; the *Rathaus* (Town Hall) is a fine building. Above the town is the Königsstuhl or King's Seat, a stone platform where between 1273 and 1400 the German Electors, so tradition has it, met to choose their king. The original "seat" was built in 1376, but the present stone dates only from 1842.

Braubach

Opposite Rhens, on the right bank of the Rhine, stands the picturesque old village of Braubach. If at all possible pay a visit here, not for the town itself, but to visit the nearby castle of Marksburg, which can be reached by a 15min walk from Braubach. This castle stands out from the numerous other Rhineland castles as it is the only one of the major medieval castles in the area that was not damaged or captured at some time or other, so it is still in its original form, an unrestored, authentic medieval feudal castle, dating from the twelfth to the fourteenth centuries, although a few additional features were added in the seventeenth. Guided tours of the castle include an extensive collection of weapons and instruments of torture, and there is a medical botanic garden.

Boppard

Boppard is one of the largest of the Rhine resorts, which boasts an elegant river promenade. There are still visible remains of the Roman town walls (*Stadtmauer*), together with a pair of Roman watchtowers. There are also medieval remains, the Binger Tor (Gate) and the Alte Burg (Castle), built by the Archbishop-Electors of Trier. The castle, which dates from both the fourteenth and seventeenth centuries, houses the Heimatmuseum.

There are two churches of note in the town, the Severuskirche and the Karmelitenkirche. The large, twin-towered Catholic Church of St Severus, located on the Marktplatz, dates from the twelfth century and is Romanesque-Gothic in style. The church, which is supposed to house the remains of Saint Severus, has beautiful thirteenth century ceiling paintings, including that of the Last Judgement, and Gothic stained glass windows. The Gothic Carmelite church, located near the Rhine promenade, has a fourteenth century Trabenmadonna statue, fifteenth century choir stalls, and a seventeenth century altar.

One of the eyesores of the region is a chairlift, located at the northern end of the town, and which ascends from the riverside to the superb Rhine viewpoint known as Vierseenblick, but RHW walkers will have no need of this service, as the trail passes here prior to its descent to Boppard. Boppard really marks the start of the true Rhine Gorge, as from here on, upriver all the way to Bingen, the scenery is

at its most dramatic. There is much to delight the rambler in the days
to come.

SUMMARY

Some may be forgiven for thinking that the RHW is not a river walk
at all, as today's route soon leaves Koblenz and the Rhine to climb up
into the surrounding countryside, not to return to the river until the
very end of the day, when the trail descends to the village of Boppard.
We are now approaching the most attractive and dramatic stretch of
the Rhine Gorge, that is the stretch between Koblenz and Bingen, but
for today we cross the Hunsrück, the hilly area to the west of the
Rhine, between the Mosel and the Nahe made famous by the *Heimat*
film and television series (for a detailed account of the Hunsrück see
"Places of Interest" in Stage 7). There is a moderate amount of ascent
and descent.

The day starts with a walk along the shore of the Rhine, out of
Koblenz, and then climbs to the Kühkopf, a prominent hill between
the Mosel and the Rhine, which at 382m is the highest point reached
on the walk so far. The route follows a Roman road, passing a couple
of Roman remains, before reaching Waldesch, a village in the heart of
the Hunsrück. Open country followed by more delightful woodland
walking leads to one of the best viewpoints of the Rhine, from
Gedeonseck above Boppard. This town, one of the largest of the River
Rhine resort villages, is reached by a very steep path which passes
beneath a cable car. The evening can be spent enjoying a relaxing
stroll along Boppard's elegant riverside promenade.

THE ROUTE

From the Deutsches Eck (German Corner), at the confluence of the
Rhein and the Mosel, where there is a huge equestrian statue of Kaiser
Wilhelm I, walk south along the left bank of the Rhine. Pass under the
road bridge and follow the walkway alongside a spur of the Rhine,
the Rhein Lache. Pass tennis courts and walk under a road bridge.
Take the right branch at a Y-junction to reach a road where you pass
under the left of the two railway arches ahead. Take the path to the left
of the road to pass under a road flyover system, a leafy and pleasant
area despite the traffic above. Immediately after crossing a small
bridge over a stream, turn right to walk under a railway bridge, cross
the road ahead (care) and walk to the left of the flyover. Within 70

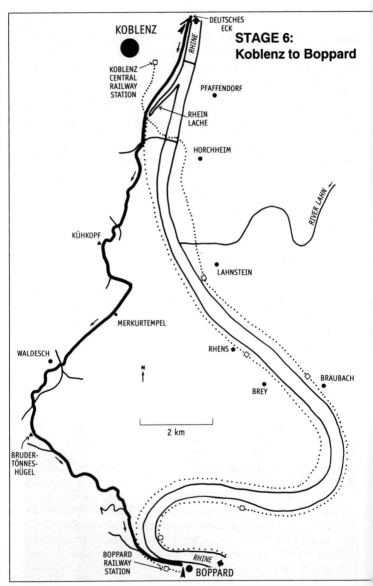

KOBLENZ

KOBLENZ
CENTRAL
RAILWAY
STATION

DEUTSCHES
ECK

STAGE 6:
Koblenz to Boppard

RHINE

PFAFFENDORF

RHEIN
LACHE

HORCHHEIM

RIVER LAHN

KÜHKOPF

LAHNSTEIN

MERKURTEMPEL

RHENS

N

WALDESCH

BRAUBACH

BREY

2 km

BRUDER-
TÖNNES-
HÜGEL

BOPPARD
RAILWAY
STATION

RHINE

BOPPARD

metres the "M" and "R" waymarked route part company. Take the left fork, remaining on the lane for the Rheinhöhenweg. Climb on this lane, but after about 350 metres leave it by taking an "R" waymarked footpath on the left (this is also for local walking routes, Nos. 1 & 3). Climb on this zigzagging path, always keeping to the main "R" waymarked trail at any junctions, to reach a metalled road, where you bear left to a small car park and Rhine viewpoint. This is Rittersturz.

A few metres south of the car park the trail splits into "RV" and "R" variants. Take the "R" waymarked trail to the right, signposted to the Kühkopf (local trail No. 1). Cross a narrow metalled lane to continue ahead on the footpath ("R" waymarks). On reaching a seat on the left (car parking area a few metres in front) turn left ("R" waymark), cross a metalled lane and continue ahead through the woods. Cross a track junction, bearing slightly to the right (bearing 210 degrees magnetic) as indicated by the "R" waymarks. The trail climbs gradually to meet a metalled lane by a small wooden shelter hut. Bear right for 30 metres to take the first turning on the left, heading uphill on a stony dirt track. The trail (local trail No. 8a) climbs to the summit of the Kühkopf, 382m. A substantial brick built shelter

A view from Gedeonseck looking south-east towards Boppard and the River Rhine

and a large cross adorn the summit, from where there is a fine view to the north of Koblenz and the Rhine and Mosel valleys. Above you is the huge radio tower which was visible from Güls.

A little concentration is required when leaving the summit, so as not to make a navigational error. Take care not to take the path waymarked with "M" paint marks, descending westwards (local route No. 8a). Instead locate a surfaced lane behind the brick shelter and follow this downhill, heading south-south-west ("R" waymarks, local route No. 9 and a "Archäologischer Wanderweg"). Descend on this lane to a T-junction, where you turn right onto an old Roman Road, heading south. After about 500 metres turn left off this lane onto a forest track ("Archäologischer Wanderweg" signpost) taking the right fork at the Y-junction. This climbs to the summit of Schullerhof, where there was once a Roman villa.

Descend slightly to a junction of five tracks. Turn right (south-west), still following the "Archäologischer Wanderweg" and "R" waymarks. Continue ahead at the next cross-tracks, signposted to Merkurtempel & Waldesch. The trail reaches a wooden shelter and the remains of Merkurtempel, a Roman temple, situated to the right of the track. After a visit to this interesting building, continue on the track (the Pastorenpfad) signposted to Waldesch. Remain ahead at a cross-tracks, but later take the left fork at a Y-junction ("R" waymarks). Continue ahead until a few metres before an open field, where you take a waymarked left fork, following the sign to Waldesch, down the left-hand side of a large field. Descend past orchards to the village of Waldesch, nestling in the valley below, passing to the left of a sports ground. Cross over the main road to enter the village.

Turn right in front of a large petrol station and then left along Koblenzer Strasse. Turn left on reaching the church onto Römerstrasse. Climb steeply on this lane. A few metres after passing Industriestrasse on the left, turn right onto a track which, within 100 metres, swings to the left. Climb on this track between fields to reach a T-junction by a metal wayside crucifix and bench. Turn left here and follow this track past a farm building to meet the main road. Turn right along this for about 300 metres, to turn left up an enclosed grassy track, beside trees. This track climbs up the field edge, aiming for a large electricity pylon. Pass under the power lines and then, at the corner of the wood

The Lorelei Rock (Stage 8)

A stream and half-timbered houses in Bacharach (Stages 8 & 9)
Vineyards stretching down to Ockenheim (Stage 10)

Boppard

(Bruder-Tönnes-Hügel, marked on the 1:50,000 map), turn left (south-east) following the sign to Jacobsbergerhof. Continue to a track T-junction where you turn left.

Keep ahead now, following the sign for Vierseenblick. At ND-Hedwigseiche (wooden shelter with table on the right) continue ahead, still following the sign to Vierseenblick. The trail reaches Engelseiche; remain on the track, following the sign for Boppard. The route finally emerges at the café-hotel-restaurant of Vierseenblick. Continue ahead, following the wooden "R" waymarks and the sign to Gedeonseck. Climb to reach a second restaurant. There is a magnificent view of a large loop in the Rhine from the terrace of this restaurant, well worth a stop for refreshments before continuing the descent into Boppard.

From the restaurant at Gedeonseck take the path heading south and signposted to Mühltal-Boppard. The trail leads to a circular shelter and another fine viewpoint of Boppard and the Rhine. The path now descends steeply beneath a chair lift. Care is required, particularly in wet weather when the rocks can be slippery. The path emerges at a couple of restaurants at a stream and waterwheel. Pass under the railway bridge to reach and cross the main road. Walk down Kreuzweg to reach the shore of the Rhine and follow the river into the centre of Boppard town.

STAGE 7
Boppard to St Goar: 25.9km (16.1 miles)

LOCATIONS	DISTANCES			
	Sectional		Accumulative	
	kms	miles	kms	miles
BOPPARD (67m; 220ft)	-	-	115.9	72.0
Point 196m near Buchenau (643ft)	5.1	3.1	121.0	75.1
SW of Fleckertshöhe (512m; 1679ft)	4.0	2.5	125.0	77.6
Karbach (460m; 1508ft)	4.3	2.7	129.3	80.3
Gründelbachtal	7.0	4.4	136.3	84.7
ST. GOAR (76m; 249ft)	5.5	3.4	141.8	88.1

FACILITIES

This section is one of the longest described in this guidebook, necessitated by the lack of accommodation between Boppard and St Goar. It would be possible to divide this stage into two very unequal sections, by an overnight stop in Bad Salzig, although this would require a detour from the RHW and would only shorten the second part of this walk to St Goar by a couple of miles. Although long, the walking is not too strenuous and there is good accommodation available at the day's end in St Goar. Those made tired by this walk can easily divide the next stage, Stage 8, into two short days.

There is not a great deal of opportunity for refreshment between Boppard and St Goar. The route does pass a café/restaurant on the outskirts of Buchenau, but this is only a few miles from Boppard at the start of the day.

Once St Goar has been reached there are no shortages of facilities, accommodation being available in a number of hotels, pensions and B&Bs. The tourist office is at Heerstrasse 120.

There is a youth hostel in St Goar at Bismarckweg 17, just outside the town centre, about a 10min walk from the railway station. The town also boasts two campsites. One (Friedenau) is in the Gründelbach valley at Gründelbachstrasse 103, passed en route; there is a restaurant on the site. The other campsite (Loreleyblick) is at An der Loreley 29-39, on the shore of the Rhine.

A ferry connects St Goar with the sister town of St Goarshausen on the right bank. Here there are hotels and guesthouses, and a little distance from the town, on the cliffs of the Lorelei to the south, is a youth hostel and a campsite. The tourist office is at Bahnhofstrasse 8.

Boats stops at Boppard, St Goar and St Goarshausen. Local train services on the left bank (Cologne to Mainz) stop at the railway stations of Boppard, Bad Salzig and St Goar, whilst those on the right bank (Cologne to Wiesbaden) stop at Kamp-Bornhofen and St Goarshausen. Local buses also operate.

MAPS

1:50,000: Der Rhein von Bingen bis Koblenz (Landesvermessungs-samt Rheinland-Pfalz).

1:25,000: Naturpark Nassau, Blatt 1 - West plus Naturpark Nassau, Blatt 4 - Süd (Landesvermessungsamt Rheinland-Pfalz).

PLACES OF INTEREST

The Hunsrück

The Hunsrück, or Hunsrück Plateau, is the huge area of volcanic schist, broad, rolling hill and woodland country lying to the west of the Rhine, between the Mosel and Nahe rivers, the latter a tributary of the Rhine into which it flows at Bingen (see Stage 9, "Places of Interest": The Nahe Valley). The upland plateau, much of it forested and dotted with numerous villages, was a relatively unknown region of Germany until the release of the 15hr award-winning film *Heimat*, the semi-autobiographical work of a local man, Edgar Reitz, set in the villages, woods and hills of the Hunsrück. The Rheinhöhenweg passes through the eastern edge of the Hunsrück, but if time is not restricted then a more thorough exploration of this tranquil, rural landscape can be recommended. The following notes should help in your travels around the Hunsrück.

The highest point of the Hunsrück is the Erbeskopf (818m; 2682ft), which is situated to the west of Idar-Oberstein (see Stage 9, "Places of Interest": The Nahe Valley). A high wooden tower stands on the Erbeskopf, from the top of which is an expansive view over the high plateau. Near here runs the Hunsrück Höhenstrasse, a scenic driving route across the plateau, a road originally built by the Nazis for military purposes. The area has been for many centuries one of the principal sources in Germany of precious stones and metal, and quarrying for them remains an important industry in the Hunsrück.

To the north of the Erbeskopf lies the town of Morbach, where

Edgar Reitz was born. His film *Heimat* tells the story of a Hunsrück family during the twentieth century, from relative poverty at the end of the Great War, to affluence by the early 1980s. The film was made entirely on location in the Hunsrück. The principal town in the film, "Schabbach", was "created" from a number of shots taken in various Hunsrück villages. Nevertheless, the precise settings of the film can be visited, and these form the basis of many touring holidays. The majority of the filming was done in three villages, Woppenroth, Gehweiler and Griebelschied, and the surrounding countryside. Woppenroth in particular is a focus for tourists: here will be found Haus Marita, named after the star of the film *Marita Breuer*, where Reitz did much of his research and wrote the film script.

Wellmich

A small village on the right bank of the Rhine, above which stands Burg Maus (see below). The village has an interesting fourteenth century church with frescoes, which is worth a look if visiting the area to view Burg Maus.

St Goar

St Goar, situated on the left bank of the Rhine, is a pleasant town; the Gründelbach valley which leads down to the Rhine and is followed by the RHW, is sylvan and particularly attractive. The principal church in St Goar, Stiftskirche, Gothic/Romanesque in style, will be found on Oberstrasse. It is worth a visit to admire the superb restored fifteenth century frescoes, located in the north aisle. There is also a doll and toy bear museum in the town.

Burg Rheinfels

Most visitors come to St Goar, however, to visit the large fortress, Burg Rheinfels, which towers above the town. The Rheinhöhenweg passes its entrance, and as it is one of the best of the Rhineland castles, a visit is strongly recommended. This massive castle complex, the largest of all the Rhine castles between Koblenz and Mainz, proved to be a virtually impregnable fortress. Built in 1245 by Count Dietrich II von Katzenelnbogen, as a means of securing tolls from passing ships, the castle was laid to siege in 1255 by an enormous force, but it held out unscathed. Later, in the sixteenth and seventeenth centuries, it was extended to form a huge fortress. It was the only Rhineland castle that the French failed to take during the War of the Palatinate

Succession. Unfortunately, at least for modern day visitors, the castle was slighted by the French in 1796. In 1845 the castle was bought by Prince Friedrich Wilhelm of Prussia. Today it is a maze of ruins and underground passages, although the medieval bulk of it remains. A museum is housed in the castle, where there is a model showing the fortress as it was in 1607, at the height of its strength and importance. There is an admission fee to the *Burg*, but this also includes entrance to the museum. (Rucksacks are usually left at reception.) The castle is normally open from 9.00 to 18.00, April to October. Allow about one and a half hours for a visit.

St Goarshausen

St Goar is linked to its sister town St Goarshausen by a ferry boat. Both towns are named after St Goar, a religious hermit who lived in Aquitaine. St Goarshausen is known as the "Lorelei Town", because of its proximity to the famous rock, which, according to the well-known legend, was home to a beautiful siren, or sea-nymph, which lured sailors to a watery grave (see Stage 8, "Places of Interest": Lorelei Rock). As might be expected, there is a prominent statue of the Lorelei in the town. It is possible to reach the top of the Lorelei cliffs by taking a path which begins in St Goarshausen (follow the signposts). A pleasant enough town, but apart from its association with the Lorelei there is little of note, although two wine festivals are held here during the autumn months.

Burg Katz and Burg Maus

Burg Katz (Cat Castle) and Burg Maus (Mouse Castle) are neighbouring feudal castles dating from the fourteenth century, located on the right bank of the Rhine in the vicinity of St Goarshausen. Burg Maus, above the small Rhine village of Wellmich, a couple of miles north-west of St Goarshausen, was the first of the two to be constructed. Built in 1355 by the Archbishop-Electors of Trier, its original name was Burg Thurnberg. The castle was destroyed in 1806, but rebuilt between 1900 and 1906. Nowadays Burg Maus houses a fine collection of raptors (eagles, falcons and other birds of prey) and displays of bird flight are given daily during the main tourist season.

The very large Burg Katz was built above St Goarshausen in 1393 by Count Johan III von Katzenelnbogen, from whom it acquired its name. It is perhaps not surprising that its rival fortress a little way downstream was soon given the name of Burg Maus. Burg Katz suffered a similar fate to its neighbouring castle, for having belonged for a considerable time to the Princes of Hessen, it was destroyed by the French in 1805, but rebuilt at the end of the nineteenth century. It is possible to visit Burg Katz by pre-arrangement with the tourist office in St Goarshausen.

Other Castles

Burg Sterrenberg and Burg Liebenstein were built "an arrow's distance apart" in the twelfth century by two brothers who hated each other, or so the story goes. They are located on the right bank of the Rhine, opposite Bad Salzig. Those taking one of the commercial Rhine boats along the river will be told in the tourist commentary the full woeful legend of the two hostile brothers.

SUMMARY

This is another fairly lengthy stage, combined with a fair amount of climbing and descent. The reason for the length of the section is the lack of accommodation between Boppard and St Goar (see comments under "Facilities" above). Anyone who may be suffering as a result of the distance should take heart in tomorrow's stage, which is shorter and can easily be divided into two very short stages.

Today's walk continues a traverse of the Hunsrück, heading principally south from Boppard, but later in the day turning east to reach the Rhine again at St Goar, over which tower the ruins of the dramatic Burg Rheinfels, in the very heart of the Rhine Gorge. The day starts with a climb out of Boppard and a gentle warm up to Buchenau, situated a little way inland, between Boppard and the riverside village of Bad Salzig. Then follows a long climb up into the wooded hills of the Hunsrück, to Fleckertshöhe, and south to the village of Karbach, at over 500m (1600ft) above sea level, the highest section so far. After a sojourn in open country the route descends to a beautiful sylvan valley. A traverse of the Frankscheid woods leads to the Gründelbach, a delightful babbling brook, which is followed on an intriguing path all the way to the Rhine at St Goar. A "must" before leaving St Goar is a visit to Burg Rheinfels, but no doubt tired walkers will leave this until the morrow, as the RHW passes the door of this most famous of Rhineland castles.

THE ROUTE

Walk along the River Promenade in Boppard to leave it at its eastern
102

end by turning right onto Michael-Bach-Strasse. Cross Mainzer Strasse and continue ahead under the railway line to turn left onto Parkstrasse. This road ends to become a footpath. Continue ahead on this footpath to reach a path junction by a telegraph pole and seat. Turn right here to climb on a zigzagging path up through the woods. Near the top of the climb turn right ("R" waymark) to walk along the left-hand edge of a field. Turn left onto the track at the top corner of the field. Ignore the next track leading off to the right, but continue ahead (south-south-east). Ignore other tracks and paths to right and left until reaching a grassy track on the right, near to an electricity pylon, about 150 metres after a Bad Salzig signpost. This track passes immediately to the left of the pylon and descends through an orchard to reach a T-junction within 200 metres. Turn left here (waymark for local footpath No. 2). The hills seen to your right across the valley are your next objective.

STAGE 7: Boppard to St Goar

Ignore the first track on the right, but on reaching a cross-tracks, turn right onto a narrow surfaced track which descends to a track T-junction at a picnic table. Turn left here and left onto the main road for about 40 metres, to turn right onto a track (waymarked "waldgaststätte"), a few metres before an electricity pylon. Keep ahead at the next track junction (ie. ignore the track on the left) and also ignore the next track on the left; climb ahead towards the wooded hills. Climb to a T-junction at the edge of the woods (232m) where you turn right following the signpost for Forsthaus and Buchenau. On reaching the café/restaurant on the outskirts of Buchenau, turn left immediately after the second large wooden shelter (the track is signposted to Pützblick). Climb into the woods on this track, following the "R" waymarks and ignoring tracks off to right and left. On reaching a cross-tracks where the track levels out, turn left, following the Rheinhöhenweg-Fleckertshöhe signpost. Climb into the woods, remaining ahead at the next cross-tracks ("R" waymarks). Continue the climb, heading south-east.

At the top of the ascent the track swings towards the south-west. Bear left, ie. maintain direction, when meeting another track. The trail heads southwards. Where the track becomes stony and starts to climb again, leave it for an "R" waymarked path on the left. (This path is also part of local trails Nos. 5 and 71.) Continue the climb, passing close to the 500m contour, maintaining direction and following the "R" waymarks to reach a main road. Cross this to follow the track opposite, signposted to Fleckertshöhe (local trail No. 9). Traffic on the nearby A61/E31 autobahn will no doubt be heard over to the right, but the motorway is never seen.

The trail enters mixed woodland and crosses open country again to reach a minor road. Cross this lane, following the signpost to the car park. Continue ahead at the next cross-tracks, following the "R" waymarks. Keep to the main track ahead, ignoring any side turnings and always following the "R" waymarks, the trail heading first in a south-south-easterly direction and then in a southerly direction. The route passes over a spot height of 532m before gradually descending. On emerging from the woods turn left (south-east), following the Rheinhöhenweg signpost, along a track between fields. Turn left on reaching a minor road to follow it for about 200 metres. Turn right onto a surfaced track (Rheinhöhenweg signpost), bearing left (south-east) at a Y-junction reached within 100 metres. Continue ahead at a cross-track, pass a wayside crucifix and descend into the Hunsrück village of Karbach.

Enter the village and descend to a crossroads, where you turn left at a Rheinhöhenweg signpost, to walk downhill to the village church. Immediately after the church turn right along Wiesenstrasse, bearing right at an electricity junction tower. Twenty-five metres after this ignore the surfaced lanes to right and left, but instead take the grit track between the two. Fifty metres later take the left fork (Rheinhöhenweg signpost - bearing of 130 degrees magnetic), thereby departing Karbach. The trail descends to the left of a stream and drops into a delightful, sylvan valley. Descend to a seat and Rheinhöhenweg fingerpost. Follow the direction of the latter to the right, descending to another bench and more fingerposts.

Cross the stream and follow the Rheinhöhenweg signpost (also local walk No. 33) steeply uphill to the right (bearing 210 degrees magnetic). After 60 metres turn left at the signpost for St Goar & Gründelbachtal (ie. leaving at this point the "R" waymarks, which continue ahead uphill). The trail heads southwards, passes a wooden hide and then bears left towards the east, so gradually climbing out of the valley. Turn right on reaching a track T-junction (Rheinhöhenweg waymarks and local walks Nos. 2 & 34). Bear left at the next track T-junction to meet a road at a hairpin bend. Do not cross this road, but bear left for 20 metres to a Y-junction, where you take the left-hand branch ("R" waymarks).

Follow this track for about 2km; it first heads eastwards, then bends to the south-east and finally to the south to reach another Y-junction. Here take the left-hand fork to reach a track T-junction within 100 metres. Turn left (south-east) here, ignoring a track on the right reached within 50 metres. Descend on the track which soon bends towards the left to head north-eastwards. Ignore the next track on the left. The trail heads north for a while, before turning to head south. On reaching a track junction turn left (east) following "Rundweg No. 34". The track soon bends to descend towards the north. Follow this main track round a hairpin bend to continue the descent, now heading south. The track eventually bends to the right to head westwards, then descending to a road.

Bear left along this road for 200 metres to turn right on a track which crosses the stream in Gründelbachtal. Bear left to take the left-hand (lower) of the two tracks which descend to the right of the river

Burg Rheinfels, St Goar

("RV" waymarks). Continue on this footpath along the right track of the stream, down the pleasant Gründelbach valley. After about 2.7km take a path on the left ("RV" waymark), which descends steeply to cross a tributary stream. Continue the descent down the Gründelbach valley to pass a campsite (access by footbridge). Remain on the footpath, which eventually passes under an archway at Pension Weingut Jacob Knab (Mühlenschenke).* The castle of St Goar is now in view. Pass through the car park of the hotel to locate a footbridge over the stream. Cross this to follow the track (grape waymark). The path climbs by a number of zigzags and then follows the right-hand side of the valley. The route passes beneath a huge rock crag, crosses a wooden bridge over a ravine, finally descending via a steep path and steps (railings) to a road. Turn right to pass under the railway bridge to reach the main road in front of the Rhine. Turn right to walk into St Goar.

* Note that a passageway, a steep narrow path and steps, links the Pension Weingut Jacob Knab (Mühlenschenke) with the Biebernheim road, 250 metres south of the entrance to Burg Rheinfels. This route could be taken by anyone wishing to bypass St Goar: the path is waymarked with a "green grape" symbol.

STAGE 8
St Goar to Bacharach: 21.1km (13.1 miles)

LOCATIONS	DISTANCES			
	Sectional		Accumulative	
	kms	miles	kms	miles
ST. GOAR (76m; 249ft)	-	-	141.8	88.1
Burg Rheinfels	0.7	0.4	142.5	88.5
Spitzestein (412m; 1351ft)	3.0	1.9	145.5	90.4
OBERWESEL (70m; 230ft)	4.2	2.6	149.7	93.0
Dellhofen (308m; 1010ft)	2.3	1.4	152.0	94.4
Perscheid (431m; 1413ft)	4.0	2.5	156.0	96.9
BACHARACH (74m; 243ft)	6.9	4.3	162.9	101.2

FACILITIES

This is one of the most popular stretches of the Rhine with visitors, and unlike the stages that precede and follow today's walk, there is easy opportunity to break the stage at approximately the half-way stage, so that the walk could be divided into two very easy half-day stages, by an overnight stop in Oberwesel. Booking accommodation is highly recommended if you intend to visit during the main holiday period.

Both Oberwesel and Bacharach have a wide selection of hotels, guesthouses and private rooms offering B&B style accommodation. Oberwesel's tourist office is at Rathausstrasse 3; Bacharach's tourist office is in the town's *Rathaus* at Oberstrasse 1, not far from the railway station. Both towns have a considerable choice of restaurants, cafés and bars, and a plentiful collection of shops, including small supermarkets. Note that the village of Dellhofen, south of Oberwesel, also boasts a supermarket and a *gasthof*/pension.

There are more youth hostels to the mile along this popular stretch of the Rhine than anywhere else in Rhineland. Apart from the hostels at St Goar and St Goarshausen (see Stage 7) there is a youth hostel en route at Oberwesel and another at the stage's end in Burg Stahleck at Bacharach, where a stay is particularly recommended for its fine location and views of the Rhine, and for its atmospheric and historical ambience. Note should be made that the hostels at both Oberwesel and Bacharach are at a considerable height above the river valley, so a steep climb is required to reach them.

There is a campsite near Oberwesel and another at Bacharach. The latter, Campingplatz Bacharach, is situated on the bank of the Rhine on Strandbadweg, a short walk south from the centre of the village. It has a good restaurant on the site. Those who venture across the Rhine to Kaub, midway between Oberwesel and Bacharach, will find a campsite (Am Elsleinband) in Blüchertal on Blücherstrasse.

There are stations for local trains at St Goar, Oberwesel and Bacharach (5-6min journeys between each station). Local buses also run fairly frequent services between these towns. Local trains on the right bank of the Rhine stop at Kaub.

MAPS

1:50,000: Der Rhein von Bingen bis Koblenz (Landes-vermessungsamt Rheinland-Pfalz).

1:25,000: Naturpark Nassau, Blatt 4 - Süd (Landesvermessungsamt Rheinland-Pfalz) plus Rheingau (HLVA).

PLACES OF INTEREST

Lorelei Rock

The Lorelei or Loreley Rock (both spellings seem to be acceptable) is undoubtedly the most famous crag in all Germany, and is associated with what is surely the most well known of all the Rhine legends. This section of the Rhine, by the 554km river marker post, has strong currents, a treacherous region for shipping, the scene of several sinkings and loss of life over the centuries. It is therefore not surprising that in superstitious medieval times the legend of the beautiful, bewitching siren or water-nymph became associated with the Rock. The Lorelei Rock was her home and here she sat, golden tresses flowing, mesmerising sailors with her beauty and mysterious, luring song, until they were dashed on the Rocks below and so sent to a watery grave.

The legend has become deeply entrenched in German culture and tradition. The first time that the Lorelei enchantress appears in print is in a poem by one Clemens Brentano, but it was the poet Heinriche Heine (1797-1856) who immortalised the Rock in the poem *Die Lorelei*, published in 1823. The words of this were later set to music and the *Lorelei Song* is played today ad nauseam on most of the tourist boats that ply this famous reach of the river.

Interestingly enough, although Heine was a Jew whose works were prohibited by the Nazis, the Lorelei poem was exempted from this ban, presumably because of its celebration of German culture and nationalism.

Those who wish to explore further can reach the top of the Lorelei cliffs by taking a path which begins in St Goarshausen.

Oberwesel

Oberwesel, on the left bank, is conveniently situated for RHW walkers, half-way between St Goar and Bacharach. This picturesque small town is surrounded by vineyards. There are two attractive churches, both worth a visit. The main church in the town, and the one most visited by tourists, is the Liebfrauenkirche (Church of Our Lady), a Gothic building known locally as the "Red Church" on account of the large sandstone blocks used in its construction. Inside there is a Baroque organ and an elaborate High Altar, also Baroque and dedicated to Saint Nicholas. But my favourite is the fourteenth century Church of St Martin (Martinskirche), which requires just a little more effort to reach as it is situated part way up a hill. The tranquillity that can be found here well repays the small exertion to reach the church. It can also be distinguished from the Liebfrauenkirche by its tower (the Liebfrauenkirche has a pointed spire). Regular organ and other concerts are held in both churches, particularly during the summer months.

Oberwesel's town ramparts are in very good condition. Sixteen defensive or watch towers dating from the thirteenth to fifteenth centuries are still standing, including the large and well-known Ochsenturm or "Ox Tower".

Schloss Schönburg

The route of the Rheinhöhenweg passes close to this castle which is above and about a kilometre south of the centre of Oberwesel. This huge, impressive medieval fortress, built by the Dukes of Schönburg, had three keeps with walls over 20ft thick, but after it was destroyed by the French in 1689 its ruins were described by Victor Hugo as the "most glorious pile of stones in Europe". Nowadays, after restoration, the complex houses a religious holiday centre and Catholic retreat, an upmarket hotel and a youth hostel. There is a wonderful view from Schönburg of the Rhine valley and surrounding Hünsruck hills.

Kaub, on the right bank of the River Rhine, with Burg Gutenfels above it

Kaub, Pfalz and Burg Gutenfels

Kaub is a village or small town, medieval in origin, situated on the right bank of the Rhine, half-way between Oberwesel and Bacharach. The medieval town walls have a parapet walk, but otherwise there is little of interest in the town itself. However, Kaub's history and its castle and Custom's House provide more than sufficient interest to warrant a visit. The building perhaps of most interest is the Pfalz or Pfalzgrafenstein Castle, located on a tiny island in the middle of the Rhine, just a little to the south of Kaub. This little white castle, built originally in 1327, with the outer walls added later, served as a toll fortress or customs tower, enabling the residents of Burg Gutenfels, who had control of this section of the Rhine, to extract taxes from passing vessels. This levying of river tolls was a highly lucrative business in days gone by, those in control of the river accumulating great wealth, but also considerable hatred from the merchants and shipowners. The practice was not confined to the medieval period, but continued well into the nineteenth century.

Burg Gutenfels originally dates from the thirteenth century. The Swedish Protestant Gustavus Adolphus was the castle's famous resident during the Thirty Years War of 1618-1648. The castle was largely destroyed by Napoleon in 1805, but partly rebuilt in the late nineteenth century, a common scenario for so many of the Rhineland castles.

The Rhine at Kaub is associated with Field Marshall Prinz Blücher von Wahlstadt, the Prussian commander who is famous for having secured victory over the French by his late arrival at the Battle of Waterloo in 1815. Eighteen months before this historic event, on New Year's Eve 1813, Blücher and his army, whilst chasing Napoleon, crossed the Rhine here by means of a military bridge constructed from materials plundered from Kaub, thereby virtually destroying the town. Today there is a museum (the Blüchermuseum at Metzgergasse 6) in Kaub, dedicated to the history of the German involvement in the Napoleonic and associated wars, which is worth a short visit. It is housed in the very same building used as Blücher's headquarters in the town. The small valley that heads north-eastwards up from the Rhine Gorge and Kaub bears Blucher's name, ie. the Blüchertal.

Bacharach

Originally known as Baccaracum, the town was named after Bacchus, the Roman God of Wine. Indeed the god's altar stone (Bacchi Ara - Bacchus's Altar) stood in the Rhine opposite Bacharach until 1850, when it was blown up to facilitate navigation in the river. But the town's origins are not Roman at all, being first mentioned in records as late as AD923. However, it does have a long association with the wine trade, dating back to medieval times, vineyard terraces covering much of the steep sided banks of the Rhine hereabouts. Bacharach also has literary associations with Heinriche Heine, who referred to it as "an ancient, sinister town" in his story of the Rabbi of Bacharach.

Picturesque Bacharach with its narrow streets and lanes, some of which are used by the RHW, and many old, attractive, half-timbered buildings, is inevitably popular, but a charming place nonetheless. The town ramparts that remain date from the fourteenth century and are well preserved. The thirteenth century town church, Peterskirche, situated on the Marktplatz, is a mixture of Gothic and Romanesque, with a fine Romanesque nave. The Church of St Nicholas is a mere 300 years old. The other religious building in Bacharach is the incomplete Wernerkapelle. A local legend, told in Heine's story of the town, concerns the supposed murder in the thirteenth century of a German boy called Werner, the act said to have been committed by Jews. The resulting pogrom was followed by plans for a shrine for the murdered boy in the form of a chapel. Built with red sandstone between 1294 and 1434, the chapel was never completed.

Of its many attractive half-timbered buildings, which date from the fourteenth to the nineteenth centuries, the Weinhaus Altes Haus, an inn built on the Marktplatz in 1368, should not be missed. But local vintages can also be enjoyed in one of the many other more modern beer cellars and bars in this wine loving town. Finally, Bacharach has its almost obligatory Rhine castle, the twelfth century but much restored Burg Stahleck, home of the twentieth century youth hostel, which the walker will pass on leaving Bacharach along the Rheinhöhenweg.

SUMMARY

A true connoisseur's day, with plenty to see and do on the way, as well as some excellent walking to enjoy. There are so many places to visit, in fact, that finding sufficient time to complete the route in one day may prove a problem. Fortunately, accommodation possibilities are such that on this section of the Rheinhöhenweg it is possible to divide the stage into two very short stages, by an overnight stop in delightful Oberwesel.

The walk starts with an ascent from the bank of the Rhine in St Goar to the entrance of Rheinfels Castle. If a visit has not already been made to this fortress, you are strongly advised to stop here now before going on, as it would be a great pity to miss one of the most imposing of the medieval Rhineland castles. There is a moderate entrance fee (for full details of the castle see "Places of Interest" in Stage 7). Next comes the ascent to the boulder-strewn summit of Spitzer Stein, a very good viewpoint, and a "real" summit, almost mountain-like. The descent from here to Oberwesel offers some of the finest views on the whole route of the Rheinhöhenweg. A lunchtime stop in Oberwesel is highly recommended, if there is insufficient time for an overnight stay - there are several restaurants. Oberwesel has two churches, with fine wall murals.

After leaving Oberwesel the trail once again climbs into the Hunsrück. The ascent to the small Hunsrück village of Perscheid is a long and often steep one, so be prepared before leaving Oberwesel.

The descent back to the Rhine from Perscheid is a real delight, down beautiful, twisting valleys, amidst an attractive tree-covered hillscape. The village of Steeg has several attractive half-timbered houses, as does Bacharach at the end of the day, now safely back on the banks of the Rhine. This is perhaps the finest section of the whole Rheinhöhenweg.

THE ROUTE
From St Goar take the road (Heerstrasse) signposted to Burg Rheinfels & Biebernheim. Climb on this road to reach the entrance to the castle, well worth a visit. Note the excellent viewpoint of St Goar reached a little before the castle. Remain on the road for about 400 metres after the *Burg* to a point where the road bends to the left. Here bear right onto the lane called Auf der Schanz (signpost to Vergissmeinnichttal). [NB: the passageway from Pension Weingut Jacob Knab (Mühlenschenke) bypassing St Goar, referred to in the footnote to the route description for Stage 7, emerges 250 metres south of the entrance to Burg Rheinfels.] Ignore the first turning on the left but follow the Auf der Schanz as it later bends to the left. Turn right onto a surfaced track opposite Friedhofsweg. Climb to pass to the right of

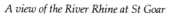

A view of the River Rhine at St Goar

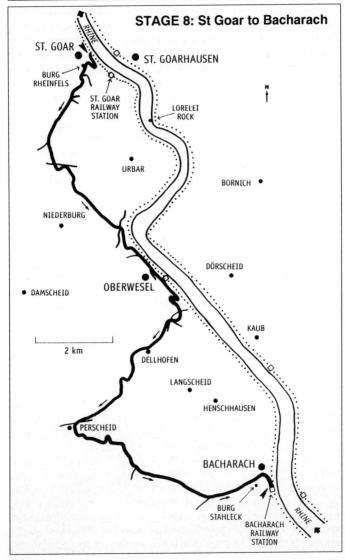

STAGE 8: St Goar to Bacharach

RHINE

ST. GOAR

ST. GOARHAUSEN

BURG
RHEINFELS

ST. GOAR
RAILWAY
STATION

LORELEI
ROCK

N

URBAR

BORNICH

NIEDERBURG

DÖRSCHEID

DAMSCHEID

OBERWESEL

KAUB

2 km

DELLHOFEN

LANGSCHEID

HENSCHHAUSEN

PERSCHEID

BACHARACH

BURG
STAHLECK

BACHARACH
RAILWAY
STATION

RHINE

a football pitch, after which the Way becomes a dirt track, traversing fields. Keep ahead at a cross-tracks to reach a road: bear right along this road for 300 metres to take a track on the right. Within 60 metres, at the edge of the wood, turn left on the track which runs alongside the wood. Follow this grassy track alongside the edge of the wood (although note that it actually enters the edge of the wood at one point), finally emerging at a track near to a small circular wooden shelter and picnic table.

Turn right (south-south-west) along the main road for 80 metres to bear left on a minor lane (arrows and "RV" painted on the ground). A hundred metres before this rejoins the main road, turn left onto a grassy/dirt track, climbing south-south-east in the woods. Continue ahead at a crossing track. Bear right at a second crossing track to reach a road within 50 metres, at this point rejoining the "R" route (ie. we have been on a variant of the Rheinhöhenweg in order to walk through St Goar - the non-variant route bypasses St Goar). Cross the road to take the forest track on the left, signposted to Spitzer Stein, now following "R" waymarks. Climb to the summit of Spitzer Stein, where there is an old stone tower, a jumble of large rocks and boulders, a seat and a fine viewpoint down to the Rhine. It is not difficult to climb the boulders to the highest point, from where the view opens out further to include the village of Niederburg.

Head north from the summit on a narrow path which descends to the road. Turn right for 10 metres, before turning right again back into the woods, continuing the descent. Keep ahead at a cross-track to descend to a track T-junction (here there is a memorial to Peter Werner and Paul Napp). Turn right for 150 metres before turning left (south) on another path. Emerge from the woods to meet a track at a T-junction (village of Niederburg ahead) where you turn left along the track. Keep ahead at a cross-tracks, the track across the fields now surfaced. A magnificent view of the Rhine Gorge around Oberwesel opens out as the trail descends to the Rheinstrasse.

Where the tarmaced track swings sharply to the right, continue ahead, downhill on the grassy track. Continue ahead at the next cross-tracks, the town of Oberwesel now clearly visible below. Continue downhill all the way to reach a road, the Rheinstrasse. Cross this to continue the descent on a narrow minor lane, soon reaching a superb viewpoint above Oberwesel. Descend through the vineyards to reach the road: turn left down this for about 200 metres

Old wine presses near Oberwesel

to the point where it swings sharply to the left at the roadsign signifying Oberwesel. Turn right here down a flight of steps (crucifix on left) to descend a steep, stony path, past a set of interesting religious murals painted on slate, to reach Koblenzer Strasse in Oberwesel. Turn right along this street to walk through Oberwesel.

Continue straight ahead along Liefrauenstrasse. On reaching the Church of Liefrauenkirche (well worth a visit) turn right up the road at its far side, signposted to the youth hostel (DJH). After about 650 metres leave the road to climb on a zigzagging footpath on the right, signposted to the youth hostel. The path emerges at a road by a car park and a wooden bridge over a gully leading to the castle. Turn left, walk through the car park, pass the youth hostel and continue along the lane to a T-junction. Turn right, uphill, for 80 metres, and then sharply to the left onto a surfaced path which soon bends to the right (good view down to Rhine). Climb to a junction, bear right (*not sharp right*) to reach a T-junction within 100 metres. Turn left here to climb on the lane into Dellhofen, entering the village on Rheinhöhenstrasse.

Pass to the right of the church and continue the ascent through the village on Rheinhöhenstrasse. Soon after leaving the village behind look out for a minor lane on the left, waymarked "R". Take this, walking south, with the hedgerow to the left and field to the right. Remain on this lane for about 800 metres to reach a cross-tracks (bench on right). Turn right (west) uphill here on a path which has an open field to the left and a hedgerow to the right. Turn left at the track T-junction at the top of the climb. After 150 metres, at a wooden watchtower, turn right alongside the right-hand edge of a field. Turn left on reaching a track T-junction (farm on right) and turn right at the next cross-tracks, at the edge of woodland. This track continues to the village of Perscheid.

Bear left on the main road in the village centre for 50 metres, to turn left onto Am Südwall (ie. taking the "RV" trail to Bacharach - at this point the "RV" trail leaves the "R" waymarked trail, which continues along the main road). Descend the steep hill to a cross-tracks, where you continue ahead, downhill, now on a grassy path. Turn left on the narrow, surfaced track reached at a T-junction. This lane descends a number of hairpin bends to lose its surface and continue as a dirt track. Follow it down into the Rindelbach valley. Descend on this trail for about 2km to reach a minor road at a hairpin bend: continue the descent ahead on this lane to reach a road T-junction. Turn left on this road (Rheingold Strasse), continuing the descent, following the stream now down the Barbach valley. Descend to the village of Steeg.

Walk along Barbach Strasse, turning right to descend to the centre of this attractive village, where there are several half-timbered buildings and a church with a turreted tower. Bear to the right in the village centre to pass to the left of the church and walk along Blücherstrasse. About 80 metres after the church turn right ("RV" waymark and "Zum Wildgehege" signboard). Ascend between houses to reach a narrow footpath which traverses the right (south) side of the valley. Continue to reach a road at a hairpin bend. Take the right fork, walking uphill. Forty metres after passing a pair of wooden telegraph poles, turn left off the road onto a descending path. On reaching a path Y-junction, take the left-hand branch, downhill. Pass under a stone gateway next to a tower and again take the left-hand path downhill. Finally descend a flight of wooden and then stone steps, to reach a track by a babbling stream in Bacharach. Turn right for the centre of the town. Pass under the Marktturm to reach the Rhine.

STAGE 9
Bacharach to Bingerbrück: 27.9km (17.3 miles)

LOCATIONS	DISTANCES			
	Sectional		Accumulative	
	kms	miles	kms	miles
BACHARACH (74m; 243ft)	-	-	162.9	101.2
Rheingoldstrasse (455m; 1492ft)	5.9	3.6	168.8	104.8
Ohligsberg (609m; 1997ft)	4.0	2.5	172.8	107.3
Lauschhütte	2.6	1.6	175.4	108.9
Salzkopf (628m; 2059ft)	0.5	0.3	175.9	109.2
Jägerhaus	5.5	3.4	181.4	112.6
Schweizerhaus	3.3	2.1	184.7	114.7
Heligkreuz	2.8	1.7	187.5	116.4
BINGERBRÜCK (83m; 272ft)	3.3	2.1	190.8	118.5

FACILITIES

The end of today's stage at Bingerbrück and Bingen offers plenty of accommodation in several cheap, and not so cheap, hotels, as well as a number of B&Bs. A full up-to-date list of accommodation can be obtained from Bingen Tourist Office at Rheinkai 21. Rüdesheim on the opposite bank of the Rhine is generally more expensive (for more details of accommodation in Rüdesheim see "Facilities" in Stage 10). Bingen Youth Hostel is located in Bingerbrück (DJH Bingen-Bingerbrück at Herterstrasse 51). Bingen has plenty of shops including several banks and a supermarket, but note that there are no shops between Bacharach and Bingerbrück.

There are no places for refreshment along the first 11 miles of today's route, but after that there are a number of café/restaurants: the Jägerhaus, the Schweizerhaus and finally the Heilig Kreuz café/restaurant, all passed en route to Bingerbrück. Bingerbrück and Bingen both have a wide choice of restaurants, cafés and bars.

There are two campsites along this section of the Rhine, both near to the river and both, unfortunately, only reached by a detour from the Rheinhöhenweg. Trechtingshausen has a campsite at Am Morgenbach 1, but those looking for a campsite at day's end will have to continue a further couple of miles along the RHW out of Bingen, before turning off for Kempten, where there is a campsite on the bank of the Rhine (see route description in Stage 10 for further details). This makes for a very long day. Alternatively, this campsite could be reached by walking eastwards from Bingen along the road which follows the shore of the Rhine to Kempten. Meals can be bought at the campsite, which can be recommended, although as it is situated close to the railway line, overnight express trains can be disturbing. There is also a campsite at Rüdesheim, on the opposite bank of the Rhine.

There are good train connections at the end of this stage with a railway station at Bingerbrück (passed en route) and another (Bahnhof Stadt Bingen) at nearby Bingen. The ferry across the Rhine from Bingen leads to the railway station at Rüdesheim for services along the right bank of the Rhine. All of the passenger boat services, up and down the Rhine, stop at Bingen.

MAPS
1:50,000: Der Rhein von Bingen bis Koblenz (Landesvermessungsamt Rheinland-Pfalz).
1:25,000: Rheingau (HLVA).

PLACES OF INTEREST
Lorch
The pleasant old village of Lorch is situated on the right bank of the Rhine, but is easily reached by ferry across from the village of Niederheimbach. Lorch was of more importance in medieval times than it is today. Many of the standard river craft were unable to cope with the rapids of the "Bingen Hole" upstream from Lorch, so many of the cargoes of the larger boats were either transferred here to smaller boats or were taken from Lorch overland to Rüdesheim. Today the village has four items of interest to the visitor: the fourteenth century Nollig Castle, a Renaissance manor, the old town walls, and the Gothic Church of Saint Martin. The latter has a Gothic High Altar and thirteenth century curved choir stalls, so is worth a visit.

Burg Sooneck
Built on a rocky outcrop above the Rhine in the twelfth century, Burg Sooneck was said to have been the most feared fortress on the Rhine. It was destroyed several times throughout its history, until finally in 1834 the ruins were purchased by Friedrich Wilhelm III of Prussia, the castle being fully restored by 1862. The fortress is open to visitors;

there is a high tower to inspect and garden terraces to enjoy. A path leads from the castle to the excellent viewpoint known as Siebenburgenblick (Seven Castle View).

Trechtingshausen and Burg Reichenstein
Trechtingshausen is a picturesque wine town above which towers the much restored Burg Reichenstein. The original castle dates from the eleventh century. It was renovated in 1834 by a certain General von Barfuss, and has in more recent times been converted into a luxurious hotel and restaurant. The establishment is open to other visitors, who may admire the various hunting trophies and armour exhibits; concerts are now held here during the main holiday season.

Burg Rheinstein
Situated a couple of miles north of Bingerbrück, perched high above the left bank of the Rhine, almost opposite the village of Assmannshausen (see below), it is possible to reach this castle on one of the commercial boat cruises from Bingen. The original fortress was built in the thirteenth century, but after considerable damage in the centuries to come, it lay in ruins until 1823 when it was bought and restored by Prince Friedrich Wilhelm of Prussia, whose body lies in the Gothic chapel of the castle. In 1975 the castle was sold to an Austrian opera singer, who restored it again and opened it to visitors. Perhaps not surprisingly there is a good view down to the Rhine from the castle.

Assmannshausen
The attractive village of Assmannshausen is of some historical significance, for it was here in 1841 that the composer Hoffman von Fallersleben wrote *Deutschland, Deutschland über Alles*. The village marks the entry into the region known as the Rheingau, a famous wine producing area which stretches from here to the outskirts of Wiesbaden (see "Places of Interest" in Stage 10).

Bingerbrück
Bingerbrück, famous for its railway yards, is really a suburb of Bingen, but is separated from the latter by the River Nahe, so that Bingerbrück and Bingen are situated on opposite sides of the Nahe valley. The two towns are connected to each other by the Drusus Bridge.

The Nahe valley

The River Nahe is a major tributary of the Rhine, flowing southwards to empty into the great river at Bingen. If time off from the Rheinhöhenweg is possible at Bingen then an exploration of this picturesque valley is recommended; this can be done by taking advantage of the train service that operates up the valley from Bingerbrück. In particular a day trip by train to Idar-Oberstein is worthwhile.

The twin town of Idar-Oberstein, situated in a rocky, wooded gorge in the Nahe valley, south-west of Bingen, is the centre for cutting and polishing precious stones, and jewellery making in the Hunsrück. The town has some good museums which detail the techniques and history of precious stone cutting and polishing. Not far away is Europe's only precious stone mine, where there are guided tours along a labyrinth of tunnels and chambers which date back to Roman times.

Bingen

Situated at the confluence of the Rhine and Nahe, Bingen is an important river port and wine centre. Although not an unattractive town, most of Bingen's houses date only from the nineteenth century. Arrival at Bingen marks the end of the most famous and dramatic section of the Rhine Gorge, nevertheless after here the river and surrounding countryside still have much to offer, and there are many interesting and attractive towns and villages still to come. There are treacherous rapids in the Rhine near Bingen, a notorious area known as the "Bingen Hole".

For the visitor the principal attraction is Burg Klopp, the large medieval type castle which dominates the town and whose high tower provides a superb viewpoint of both rivers and of the Hünsruck and Taunas hills. The *Burg* was the fortress of the Bishop-Electors of Mainz. The original castle, built in the thirteenth century on the foundations of a Roman fort, was largely destroyed in 1689, with further damage inflicted in 1711. The present building is a replica of the original and dates, like so many of the Rhineland castles, from the nineteenth century. The castle today houses a Heimatmuseum, a local history museum exhibiting prehistoric artifacts, ancient weapons, and the like (open daily, except Mondays, 9.00-12.00 and 14.00-17.00, small entrance fee). The *Rathaus* (Town Hall) and other administrative offices are also housed within the castle buildings.

The other main building of interest in the region is the Mäuseturm or Mouse Tower, an old custom's tower situated on a small rocky island in the Rhine. There are three possible origins for its rather unusual name. The more prosaic is that the name comes from the verb *mausen*, to spy. This seems quite plausible as the function of the tower, built during the thirteenth century, was basically to keep tabs on shipping passing up and down the Rhine (although it was also probably used as an armoury). A second theory, equally mundane, is that the name refers neither to espionage nor to rodents, but to *maut*, ie. custom's money, which was levied here. However, tour guides prefer to relate the gory legend with which the tower is also associated. The story is that one Archbishop Hatto of Mainz, after having starving local peasants burned alive during a famine, received divine retribution by being eaten alive by mice in the Mäuseturm.

Two religious buildings are of interest in Bingen. The Basilika Saint Martin in Bingen was built in the eighth century on the ruins of a Roman temple. The Chapel of Saint Rochus, which has an interesting Romanesque crypt, was built in 1666 on a hilltop to the east of the town. Every August the Rochus festival is held at this small church to celebrate the life of Saint Rochus, who is said to have saved the town from the Black Death during the Middle Ages.

SUMMARY

The section between Bacharach and Bingerbrück, at over 17 miles, is the longest stage of the whole Rheinhöhenweg, and the day is made even longer if you continue to cross the River Nahe to enter Bingen. This is necessitated by the lack of accommodation in this southern end of the Hunsrück, although at journey's end in Bingerbrück/ Bingen there is an abundance of accommodation. Moreover, you must be completely self-sufficient for the first 11 miles of the trail after leaving Bacharach as there are no refreshments until the Jägerhaus café/restaurant. It is important to take sufficient food and drink with you for the day.

The walk today is also reasonably strenuous as the route climbs to the highest point reached on the whole of the Rheinhöhenweg, ie. to the 628m (2059ft) high Salzkopf, on whose summit will be found a 24m (79ft) high watchtower, which allows a fine view above the trees of the Hunsrück hills. Despite its length and undulating nature, this stage, like most of the Rheinhöhenweg, offers no real difficulties and should be well within the capabilities of the average rambler. Once this section has been accomplished you can take heart as the remaining stages are all much shorter and easier.

The day starts with a climb up to the impressive Burg of Bacharach, now a youth hostel, after which there is a long walk along an old Roman Road. This first section of the day offers a small taste of another European ultra-long distance "E-route", ie. the E 3. Then follows a long traverse of the extensive Bingen forests. A traverse of the Ohligsberg is followed by an ascent to the Salzkopf, which as well as being the RHW's highest point, is also a good place for a lunch stop. After the Salzkopf there is a long gradual descent through the woods to Jägerhaus where there is a café/restaurant. Here our Rheinhöhenweg leaves the E 8 European long distance path, which it has followed for a large part of the route since Bonn. The E 8 has a great deal further to run than our humble RHW, as it is heading for Hungary, but this is the last time the Rheinhöhenweg and the E 8 coincide. From the Jägerhaus there is an agreeable stroll down the valley known as Margenbachtal, beside a pleasant babbling brook. The trail then approaches the Rhine again, and from the terrace at Schweizerhaus (another café/restaurant) there is a superb view of the river and of Assmannshausen and Bingen. A slow descent towards the south leads eventually to Bingerbrück, where the Nahe is crossed to reach the large and well-known town of Bingen, which signifies the end of this attractive and dramatic section of the Rhine Gorge.

THE ROUTE
From the church in Bacharach take the road signposted to Steeg. After 100 metres fork left, following the signpost for the "Jugendherberge", walking alongside a brook. Eighty metres later climb the steps on the left ("RV" and "Jugendherberge" signs). Up until this point the walk has merely been the reverse of the inward route to Bacharach, but now, on reaching a path junction, do not turn right ("RV" waymark), but continue ahead (east) following the waymark for local walks Nos. 3 and 4. Ignore the first turn on the right (signposted as route No. 1), but take the second on the right, up a flight of stone steps. This path climbs steeply by a number of zigzags, and carries a "blue cross" waymark (that of the E 3 International Long Distance Path). Climb to pass under the stone archway of the impressive Burg Stahleck, which

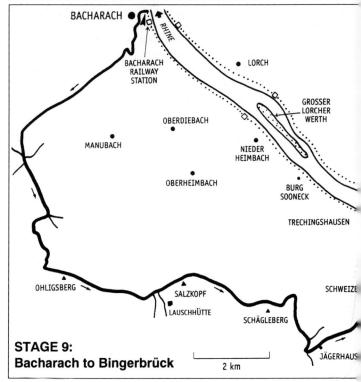

BACHARACH

RHINE

LORCH

BACHARACH
RAILWAY
STATION

OBERDIEBACH

GROSSER
LORCHER
WERTH

MANUBACH

NIEDER
HEIMBACH

OBERHEIMBACH

BURG
SOONECK

TRECHINGSHAUSEN

OHLIGSBERG

SALZKOPF

SCHWEIZE

LAUSCHHÜTTE

SCHÄGLEBERG

**STAGE 9:
Bacharach to Bingerbrück**

JÄGERHAUS

2 km

now serves as the town's youth hostel. Fifty metres after the wooden
bridge that spans a gully at the hostel, bear left onto a footpath ("blue
cross waymarks") which leads to a road at a hairpin bend. Turn left
uphill on the road (signpost to Neurath). Do not take the left fork
within 100 metres ("grape" waymark symbol), but continue climbing
on the road for about 600 metres, until you reach picnic tables and a
dirt track on the right-hand side of the road. Take this track to climb
above the village of Neurath.

Turn right on reaching a T-junction, continuing the ascent, now
on a narrow surfaced lane, which at first heads northwards and later
swings to the left to head south-west. This is an old Roman road. It
climbs for a while, eventually losing its surface to become a dirt track
124

(at this point ignore another track on the right), after which the walking is more or less on the level. Eventually, after about 3km the main track swings to the right by the edge of a conifer plantation. Leave the main track here, instead continuing ahead on another track, to the left of the conifer wood. Continue on this track to reach a metalled road (Rheingoldstrasse). At this point the "R" waymarked standard route of the Rheinhöhenweg is rejoined.

Cross the road to continue ahead on the track heading south ("blue cross" and "R" waymarks). After 150 metres, at a Y-junction, take the left-hand branch (the E 3, "blue cross" waymarks takes the right-hand branch here), still heading south. Keep ahead, ignoring other tracks to right and left, until three sets of overhead power cables are reached at three large pylons. Turn right at this point onto a track that soon crosses a grassy field. Bear left in front of the wood at the far side of this field, now heading south. After about 400 metres, at a gate, fence and a very small wooden building, turn left along the left-hand edge of a field for 100 metres, and then right along a path *between* trees. Continue ahead when another track joins from the left. On reaching a junction of six tracks continue ahead (bearing 155 degrees magnetic), following the "R" waymarks. Turn right at the next cross-

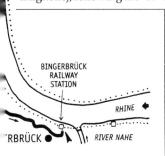

tracks, climbing to the south-west. Bear left on reaching a Y-junction (fence and buildings on the right), continuing to climb. Continue the ascent, ignoring any side turnings, following "R" waymarks, walking east-south-east over the Ohligsberg.

On reaching a wooden finger-post on the Ohligsberg, continue ahead, following the signpost to Lauschhütte, 2.5km (and 14.5km on the "R" route to Bingen). At HT electricity cables remain ahead over a cross-track to pass under the cables and continue ahead, following the "R" waymarks. The trail leads to a road at a car park and houses: follow the road ahead for 100 metres, before bearing left at a signpost for Salzkopfturm and Jägerhaus. Head east-north-east up this track to reach the summit of Salzkopf (628m). The summit is 50 metres to the right of the main path. There is a huge watch tower (24m high) on the summit as well as a wooden shelter, which would be most welcome in bad weather. Climb up the tower for a fine view above the trees of the Hunsrück hills.

Begin the descent on the main path. After about 750 metres a junction is reached, which is situated by a picnic table. The "RV" variant goes off to the left. Ignore this but instead continue ahead on the "R" waymarked trail. Continue ahead (signpost Jägerhaus) at the next track junction, and remain ahead at the next cross-tracks to descend. Continue to follow the "R" waymarks on the descent through the forest. At Schägle the track bends to the north. On reaching a cross-tracks at a seat and fingerpost, turn right (south), signposted to Jägerhaus, 1.5km (ie. it is most important here to take this right turn and not continue straight on, signposted "Rundweg Jägerhaus"). When the Jägerhaus (café / restaurant) is reached, bear right to walk downhill on a lane which leads to a bridge over a stream.

Immediately after the bridge turn left (signpost to "Trechtinghausen Nr. 9") on a track which descends to the right of the stream. After 150 metres, the E 8, which has been our route for much of the way since Bonn, leaves you for the final time by taking a right turn up a path by the side of a tributary stream. You continue straight ahead on the track down Morgenbachtal. After about 1.7km leave the river by turning right at a small, wooden shelter. Climb to a cross-track and then continue ahead, now on a level path, but soon descending to pass over a cross-track. Continue ahead, quite steeply downhill, following "R" and "IVV" waymarks, and a fingerpost indicating Schweizerhaus, 0.3km and Bingen, 5.8km. Pass a stone monument on the left dated 1836 and continue to Schweizerhaus, a café and restaurant. It is worth taking refreshment on the terrace of this establishment, to enjoy the superb view of the Rhine, Assmannshausen opposite, and Bingen to the south.

Bear right on a track in front of the Schweizerhaus, signposted "Heiligkreuz Nr. 4". After about 400 metres, take a descending path on the left ("R" and "IVV" waymarks). Descend around the head of a delightful woodland gorge and about 150 metres later take a right, "R" waymarked fork, at a signboard indicating "Gaststätte Heilig Kreuz". Climb gradually on this balcony path, heading south, with occasional views down to the River Rhine below. At the top of the climb continue ahead, over crossing paths, still following "R" and "IVV" waymarks. The path eventually emerges at the Heilig Kreuz café / restaurant.

Turn left onto the lane. After about 350 metres, where the road forks, take the left-hand branch ("no entry for vehicles" roadsign). After 80 metres bear right onto a path which parallels the road, a little above and to its right. The trail descends, eventually reaching a wooden shelter at a viewpoint over the Rhine. Continue the descent, now on a narrow, surfaced lane (note that at this point the route joins the 1:50,000 map "Mainz und Rheinhessen"). Where a surfaced drive leaves the road on the left (opposite a sign pointing backwards and indicating "Fussweg zum Bingen Wald"), take this drive to descend to Prinzenkopfstrasse, on the outskirts of Bingerbrück. Descend on this road to reach a main road in the centre of Bingerbrück. Turn left along this road for 80 metres to locate steps, just beyond a car park on the right. Cross the footbridge over the railway lines to arrive at the railway station.

Turn right, following the sign for the "Stadtmitte" (town centre). Cross the bridge over the River Nahe, so leaving the Hunsrück, to enter Bingen.

A group of German walkers at Salzkopf

STAGE 10
Bingerbrück to Ingelheim: 16.6km (10.3 miles)

LOCATIONS	DISTANCES			
	Sectional		Accumulative	
	kms	miles	kms	miles
BINGERBRÜCK (83m; 272ft)	-	-	190.8	118.5
BINGEN (128m; 420ft)	1.0	0.6	191.8	119.1
Hildegardhaus	1.9	1.2	193.7	120.3
Ockenheim (110m; 361ft)	5.1	3.2	198.8	123.5
Jakobsberg (chapel)	1.5	0.9	200.3	124.4
Gau-Algesheim	2.2	1.3	202.5	125.7
Bismarckturm	2.4	1.5	204.9	127.2
INGELHEIM-SÜD (Burgkirche)	2.5	1.6	207.4	128.8

FACILITIES

There is a hotel-restaurant and a *gasthof* in the village of Ockenheim at the half-way stage of today's journey. Ingelheim-Süd has at least one pension, and there is a hotel in the main town of Ingelheim itself.

Obtaining accommodation at the end of today's stage may be a little more difficult than on previous days. If in difficulty you could take a train from Ingelheim back to Bingen for a second night in a hotel there, or on to Mainz where there is abundant accommodation.

Those wishing to explore the north bank of the Rhine in this area will find accommodation in both Rüdesheim am Rhein and in Geisenheim. Rüdesheim has many hotels and several pensions/*gasthofen*, as well as a youth hostel, although the latter is some way from the centre of the town, a walk of over a kilometre (see Appendix A). Rüdesheim's tourist office is at Rheinstrasse 16. Geisenheim also has accommodation, details of which can be sought from the tourist office at Rüdesheimerstrasse 48. Campers seeking accommodation on the right bank are spoilt for choice: there are two campsites in Rüdesheim, one of which (Campingplatz am Rhein) is located on the banks of the Rhine. Geisenheim's campsite is also situated by the river. There are campsites on the left bank at Kempten (see "Facilities" in Stage 9) and at Ingelheim-Nord, although note that the latter is over 5km off-route.

There are a few places where refreshment may be obtained en

The restored tower and part of the old town walls near the
Burgkirche, Ingelheim-Süd (Stages 10 & 11)
The Dom,Mainz (Stages 11 & 12)

route (these are mentioned in the route description below). These include the village of Ockenheim at the half-way stage (restaurant and a supermarket) and the Bismarckturm, where there is a a café/restaurant adjacent to the tower. There are several shops in Ingelheim-Süd and cafés and restaurants in Ingelheim.

MAPS
1:50,000: The entire stage from Bingerbrück to Ingelheim is covered by the map "Mainz und Rheinhessen" (Landesvermessungsamt Rheinland-Pfalz). The first half of the route, from Bingerbrück to a couple of kilometres east of Ockenheim, is included on the map "Der Rhein von Bingen bis Koblenz" (also Landesvermessungsamt Rheinland-Pfalz).
1:25,000: Rheingau plus Wiesbaden und Umgebung (HLVA).

PLACES OF INTEREST

Bingen
For full details see "Places of Interest" in Stage 9.

Hildegard's House (Hildegardhaus) - Hildegard of Bingen
Hildegardhaus can be visited by a short detour from the trail on the eastern outskirts of Bingen. Bingen's most famous resident, an abbess and mystic, Hildegard lived here during the twelfth century. Known as the "Sybil of the Rhine" she experienced visions from childhood, accounts of which she wrote in the manuscript known as the *Scivias*, begun in 1141. She was born in 1098 at Bermersheim in Rheinhessen, the last child of a family of ten. She entered an Enclosure in 1106, taking her vows and receiving the veil in 1112. She took over the community of nuns in 1136, which she developed into one of the major communities in this part of Europe and, though suffering from serious illnesses for many years, went on several adventurous preaching tours, each lasting for several years. She eventually died in 1179 at the age of 81, a very long lived woman for those times. Surprisingly she was never canonised.

Rheingau
The region on the northern side of the Rhine, between Lorch and Wiesbaden is known as the Rheingau. In this area the Rhine flows

A stone tower, Burg Oppenheim (Stages 13 & 14)

Rüdesheim

generally in a westerly direction. The Rheingau is one of the principal wine growing areas of Germany; Rheingau Riesling is particularly famous. A great many vineyards dot this rural landscape which also, perhaps not surprisingly, boasts a considerable number of ruined Romantic medieval castles. A walking trail, the Rheingauer Riesling Pfad, is a must for wine fans. It runs through the vineyard covered hill country of the Taunus.

Burg Ehrenfels
This castle, once a toll castle used to control traffic on the river below, is situated on the right bank of the Rhine. It was built between 1208 and 1220 by the Archbishop of Mainz, but alas is now in ruins. In times of war the treasures of Mainz Cathedral were stored here for safe-keeping.

Rüdesheim am Rhein
Rüdesheim is situated on the right bank of the Rhine opposite Bingen and is well worth a visit by those with time available (it is easily reached from Bingen by ferry). The town is very popular with tourists, a fact which is reflected in its generally high prices. It is an attractive town, with many sixteenth to eighteenth century merchants'

130

and noblemen's half-timbered houses, and narrow, medieval streets, often very congested during the summer months. The main street is the Drosselgasse. Two interesting medieval noblemen's houses open to visitors are the Bröserhof (this houses a collection of musical instruments) and the half-timbered Klunkardshof. Four castles once guarded Rüdesheim, one of which, Brömserburg, remains and is one of the oldest fortresses on the Rhine. Built by the Knights of Rüdesheim on the site of an earlier Roman fortification, Brömserburg is particularly worth visiting as it houses the excellent Rheingau and Wine Museum. This details the history of this area of the Rhine from Roman times to the late Middle Ages and also contains a large collection of wine presses and other equipment relating to grape growing and wine production. Also of interest in Rüdesheim is the Boosenburg, a twelfth century defensive tower, the Adlerturm, a circular late Gothic tower, and a Gothic church. There is a fireworks display in Rüdesheim at the beginning of July and a Wine Festival in mid-August: on both occasions finding accommodation can be difficult.

Niederwald Memorial Statue

This large monument, the Niederwalddenkmal, also known as the Germania Memorial Stone, was built in 1871 from a large number of old Prussian cannons, to commemorate the recent unification of the German states, and erected here in 1883. At the unveiling ceremony in the same year there was an unsuccessful attempt to assassinate the Kaiser. The monument, 40m high, stands 225m above Rüdesheim, at a really superb viewpoint, which can be reached either on foot up a steep path or by chairlift (the lower chairlift station is only a few minutes' walk from the Drosselgasse).

Geisenheim

A few miles to the east of Rüdesheim, this is another attractive town on the right bank which is well worth a visit. The town is associated with the best wines in the area, the Riesling in particular being of a very high quality. The town boasts the National Research Station for Wine, Viticulture and Horticulture. Apart from the many half-timbered houses to admire there is the eighth century Rheingau Cathedral to visit, as well as a number of castles.

Of these the sixteenth century Schloss Schönborn is of the most historical significance. It was in this castle that Johann Philipp von Schönborn, Elector and Archbishop of Mainz, negotiated the peace of

Westphalia which brought to an end the European Thirty Years War. Schloss Johannisberg is situated north-east of Geisenheim. Built in the eighteenth century, on the site of a twelfth century abbey, it is owned by the Metternich family: there are good views of the Rhine from this castle.

Oestrich-Winkel
This small town is situated on the Rhine opposite Ingelheim. The town boasts not only what is said to be the oldest stone house in Germany, the ninth century Gray House (Graues Haus) which is nowadays an expensive restaurant, but also the oldest (twelfth century) parish church in the Rheingau. Also of interest is Brentano House, which dates from 1751, where there is a collection of the works of Goethe and various Romantic poets. Finally, the town has a unique sixteenth century wooden crane. Situated to the north of Oestrich-Winkel is the fourteenth century Schloss Vollrads, one of the best preserved medieval fortresses in the Rheingau.

Bismarckturm
This monumental stone tower, the Bismarckturm, is passed on the RHW, west of Ingelheim-Süd. Thirty-one metres in height, it provides a very good viewpoint. It was erected in 1902 to commemorate the German Chancellor, Otto von Bismarck (1815-1898), who played a decisive role in bringing about the unification of the German states to form the Second German Reich in 1871. The tower is open from April to September, 9.00-20.00, and October to March, 10.00-16.00.

Ingelheim
Known as the Red Wine Town, Ingelheim was the site of the former Imperial Palace of Charlemagne. The palace has now disappeared, along with the town's former importance: in 1105 it witnessed the Ingelheim Royal Congress, which set up an alliance of the Bishops of Mainz, Worms and Koblenz, which ousted the Emperor Heinrich IV. The most famous Ingelheim resident was one Sebastian Münster, a sixteenth century astronomer who drew some notable star charts. The town today is noted for the high quality of its asparagus.

SUMMARY
At Bingen the Rhine, which has been heading generally in a south-easterly direction all the way from Cologne, makes a large turn to

head eastwards towards Mainz and Wiesbaden. The Rheinhöhenweg, although, as always, rarely following the banks of the great river, nevertheless follows its general course, and so too turns eastwards to follow footpaths and tracks to reach the town of Ingelheim, mid-way between Bingen and Mainz. This forms the route of today's stage. Woods have formed a prominent feature of the landscape on our journey south from Bonn. Now woods are to become much less frequent, giving way instead to more open country amidst vineyards. The landscape becomes less harsh from now on, gentle rolling hill country.

The Nahe valley is crossed to walk through the town of Bingen. The streets of Bingen are soon replaced by vineyards and gentle rolling hills lead to a number of pleasant, interesting villages and small towns including Ockenheim and Gau-Algesheim. The impressive Bismarkturm is visited en route between Gau-Algesheim and Ingelheim, the end point of today's stage. In the more attractive southern part of the town, Ingelheim-Süd, through which the RHW passes, is the Burgkirche, an impressive building whose stout walls have been attractively restored.

THE ROUTE
From the railway station turn right, following the sign for the "Stadtmitte" (town centre). Cross the bridge over the River Nahe, so leaving the Hunsrück, to enter Bingen. Follow the Fruchtmarkt and then the Rheinstrasse, to turn right along a pedestrianised shopping street. Turn left along Speisemarkt. A few metres after the church on the left, turn right along Am Burggraben (signpost to Burg Klopp). At the top of this road bear left through a stone archway to climb a flight of steps on the right. Climb the walkway ahead and then turn right up a second flight of steps, immediately turning left up more steps to pass the Burg Klopp restaurant, near the Heimatmuseum. Walk through another stone archway and then a third archway to arrive at Maria-Hilf-Strasse. Turn left along this street to descend to a T-junction, where you turn right, uphill (signpost Rochusberg). Follow this road out of town, continuing along Rochusallee.

On reaching the edge of woods, by a shrine, turn left onto an "R" waymarked *fussweg*. On reaching a "Y" path junction, bear right uphill. Continue ahead uphill at the next cross-paths. Emerge back on the road and continue uphill. On reaching a crossroads by a vineyard (café-restaurant 100 metres to the right), continue ahead through the vineyards on the Rochusweg. Those seeking the campsite at Kempten should turn off on a path heading north through the vineyards to reach the outskirts of the town: the campsite is situated on the banks of the Rhine, near to the railway line, and is about a mile off the RHW.

The trail descends to cross a bridge over the spur of the A60 (E42) autobahn. On the other side of the bridge there is a junction of five tracks/lanes. Bear slightly left (*not* sharp left) to continue (bearing 130 degrees magnetic) on a narrow, surfaced track through the vineyards. Cross a second bridge over the A60 (E42) motorway, and then a third, this time over a railway bridge. At the far side of this bridge take the left fork. Cross a fourth bridge, again over a railway line, and continue ahead (ignore track on right) through the vineyards. Where this lane swings sharply to the right, leave it to walk ahead (bearing 80 degrees magnetic) with a vineyard to your left and a line of trees to your right. On reaching a crossroads (bridge to left over railway) turn right along the road, heading along Gaulsheimer Strasse into the village of Ockenheim.

After 500 metres ignore the road on the right, signposted to Bingen-Büdesheim, but swing with the road to the left, heading for the centre of Ockenheim. Head through the village along Bahnhofstrasse, passing immediately to the right of the church to reach a T-junction at Mainzer Strasse. Turn right (direction Bad Kreuznach) for 60 metres to turn left along Bergstrasse (signpost "zum St. Jakobsberg"). After 250 metres bear left, still following the signs to Jakobsberg. Climb on this lane, passing a number of houses, to reach a picnic table and benches on the left-hand side of the road. Turn left here on a surfaced track, climbing through vineyards. There is an expansive view to the left of Ockenheim and Caulsheim. After 350 metres, at a cross-track, bear right, uphill on a grassy track, heading for houses.

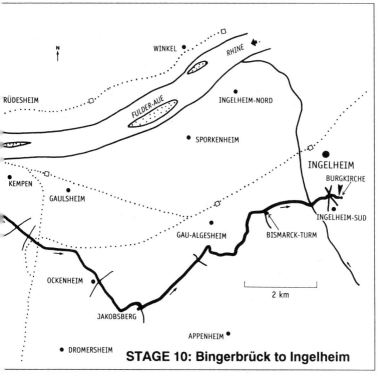

STAGE 10: Bingerbrück to Ingelheim

Bear left at the T-junction onto a lane, passing a "virgin with Christ". After about 150 metres, at a bench and shrine, climb a long flight of wooden steps on the right, to reach the church of St. Jakobsberg (worth a visit). Bear left in front of the church to follow a track heading east-north-east ("R" waymark and local footpath No. 1). After 750 metres ignore a track down to the left, but continue ahead, now on a surfaced track. (Note that at this point the RHW runs off the 1:50,000 scale map entitled "Der Rhein von Bingen bis Koblenz".) Ignore all side tracks and paths, descending ahead, aiming for the prominent church steeple of Gau-Algesheim, seen below.

Turn right on reaching a T-junction and in 50 metres left over a bridge spanning a main road. At the far side of the bridge ignore route

No. 1 on the left, but continue ahead towards the houses. Walk along the residential street (Im Blätterweg) to the T-junction at Saulieustrasse. Turn right for 50 metres and then right again (south) on Caprino-Veronese-Strasse. Continue to a T-junction where you turn left downhill to a second T-junction: here turn left for 50 metres and then right down a flight of steps on In Der Stolzwiese. Turn left in front of a stream and after 50 metres, at a T-junction by a children's play area, turn right (bearing 110 degrees magnetic) along An Der Layenmühle. Ignore Kaiser-Karl-Strasse on the left, but take the next left (Im Hippel). Climb on this road for about 350 metres until, opposite Im Bangert, turn right, uphill, on a surfaced drive. Within 25 metres bear right to join a grassy track (vineyard on right). Climb to cross over a cross-track and continue the ascent, heading north-north-east. Later ignore a signposted track on the right to Appenheim, but bear left at the next fingerpost, signposted to Bismarckturm. Continue to a viewpoint shelter on the left (a good view down to Gau-Algesheim) and a metal cross on the right. Here bear right on a narrow footpath, signposted to Ingelheim, 3.5km.

Bear right on reaching a path T-junction, now heading south. Turn left on meeting another track (gate to right) continuing to a T-junction (good view ahead to Ingelheim-Süd), where you turn left to reach the monumental stone tower, the Bismarckturm. There is a café/restaurant adjacent to the tower and the site affords a panoramic viewpoint of the valley and of Ingelheim below.

Leave the Bismarckturm by descending northwards, to the right of the tower, but only for 50 metres, where a track T-junction will be encountered. Turn right here. Descend to another track T-junction, where you bear right through vineyards. Bear right on reaching a narrow lane (*not* the track sharp right) to continue the descent on this lane to reach the outskirts of Ingelheim-Süd. Cross the bridge over the river and walk along Altengasse (a shop and a pension will be passed on the way). The road climbs gently to reach Stiegelgasse; here bear left to reach a major crossroads (several shops will be found here). Cross over to walk along An Der Burgkirche. Walk under a stone arch to reach the impressive church of Ingelheim-Süd, the Burgkirche.

STAGE 11
Ingelheim to Mainz: 21.8km (13.5 miles)

LOCATIONS	DISTANCES			
	Sectional		Accumulative	
	kms	miles	kms	miles
INGELHEIM-SÜD (Burgkirche)	-	-	207.4	128.8
Heidesheim (106m; 348ft)	7.2	4.5	214.6	133.3
Lenneberg Palace	5.9	3.6	220.5	136.9
Nothelferkapella (Gonsenheim)	1.8	1.1	222.3	138.0
MAINZ (Town Centre)	6.9	4.3	229.2	142.3

FACILITIES

Mainz is a major tourist and commercial city and as such has a large number of hotels of all star ratings, as well as numerous guesthouses. There is a large youth hostel (see Appendix A) but this is situated some way out of the city centre (a little over 2km to the south-east, to the west of the Rhine). The city campsite (recommended) is located on the right bank and is reached on foot by walking across the Theodor Heuss Brücke: on the far side turn right; the campsite is about 700 metres to the south-east, on the far side of the Flosshafen. The tourist office (Verkehrs-Verein) is opposite Mainz Haupt Bahnhof (main railway station) on Bahnhofstrasse. Note that there is also a youth hostel in neighbouring Wiesbaden (see Appendix A).

Shops of all types, including large supermarkets and several department stores, will be found in Mainz, as well as an abundance of cafés and restaurants, from the simplest snackbar to *haute cuisine*. There is an excellent city bus and tram service, and of course mainline train services south to Mannheim, north-east to Frankfurt and north-west to Cologne. The main railway station has a computer information system. Finally Rhine pleasure boats leave at frequent intervals from the bank near the *Rathaus* (Town Hall) where the KD Line offices will also be found.

En route one café/restaurant is passed a little after Heidesheim, just to the south of the A60/E42 autobahn.

There are two principal alternatives to Mainz for accommodation in this area. First, there is the town of Eltville am Rhein on the right bank of the river, where there are several hotels. The town is on the main Frankfurt to Cologne railway line. The tourist office is at Schmittstrasse 2-4.

Second, the neighbouring city of Wiesbaden is easily reached from Mainz by train or bus, has plenty of hotels, and is well worth a day's visit if time is available (see "Places of Interest" in Stage 12). The main railway station (*Hauptbahnhof*) in Wiesbaden is a little south of the city centre. There is a tourist office in the *Hauptbahnhof* and another at Rheinstrasse 15. Bear in mind that hotels here tend to be on the expensive side. There is also a youth hostel in Wiesbaden at Blücherstrasse 66. Note that Mainz and Wiesbaden have an integrated public transport network which allows travel within and between the two cities on one ticket; enquire for details at the main railway stations in either Mainz or Wiesbaden.

MAPS

1:50,000: Mainz und Rheinhessen (Landesvermessungsamt Rheinland-Pfalz).

1:25,000: Rheingau plus Wiesbaden und Umgebung (HLVA).

PLACES OF INTEREST

Rhein-Hessen

The area around Mainz, extending west towards Bingen and south to Worms, is known as Rhein-Hessen. The area is extensively covered in vineyards and is principally known for its huge viticulture industry. The remainder of the walk along the RHW to Mainz, Oppenheim and Alsheim is within this region.

Trullos

Trullos are small, conical, white shelters used by vineyard workers and often situated within the vineyards. They are unique to this region of Germany. Apart from this area they are only found elsewhere in the Italian region of Apulia. It is thought that they were built in the mid-nineteenth century by Italian immigrants. Unfortunately no trullo is seen on the actual route of the RHW through Rhein-Hessen, but you can see one of these unique buildings by a short detour in Heidesheim, where about 150 metres off-route a trullo has been converted into a private house.

Eltville am Rhein

Situated in the centre of the Rheingau, on the right bank of the Rhine,

A 'trullo' converted to a house in Ingelheim

to the north-west of Mainz, the town of Eltville am Rhein has a history stretching back to Roman times. Eltville is well known amongst Germans for the production of Sekt, a German sparkling wine, very similar to champagne. In German literature it is the town where Thomas Mann's fictional character Felix Krull spent his youth. Historical interest comes from the fact that Johann Gutenberg (1400-1468), inventor of the printing press, was a member of the court at Eltville. Apart from the many attractive half-timbered buildings, there is a castle and a gothic church. Eltville Castle was built by the Archbishop of Trier from 1330, but only the fifteenth century keep remains today. The fourteenth century Gothic Parish church of Saints Peter and Paul has fourteenth century stained glass and fifteenth century frescoes on the ceiling.

In the nearby village of Kiedrich, 3km to the northwest of Eltville, and easily reached by bus, is one of the oldest working church organs in Germany, dating from around 1500, housed within the splendid fifteenth century church of St Valentinus.

Mainz

The allocation of at least one full day is strongly recommended to explore Mainz, capital of the Rhineland-Palatinate and the major Rhineland city passed en route.

The city, strategically situated at the confluence of the Rivers Rhine and Main, has a long history dating back to Roman times. It was created a Bishopric in AD 742 by Saint Boniface, becoming a principal centre for Christianity in northern Europe. The city became the capital of the League of Rhenish Cities in 1254, so assuring its economic and political pre-eminence. During the Middle Ages the Elector Archbishop of Mainz became one of the most powerful princes within the Holy Roman Empire. During the Napoleonic Wars the city was captured by the French, after which it was known for a time as Mayence. Mainz is famous as the birthplace of Johannes Gutenberg, the developer of printing in Europe, who, incidentally, as a result went bankrupt.

If you only have time to visit one building in Mainz, make it the cathedral or dom, which is passed en route in the centre of the city. The first cathedral on this site was built at the end of the tenth century, but this lasted but a very short time, as it was burnt down in 1009 on the day of its consecration/dedication. The present cathedral was dedicated in 1036 and completely finished by the end of the eleventh century, but there have been significant structural and decorative changes throughout the ages and substantial parts were rebuilt after World War Two. One of the principal buildings of Mainz, the cathedral celebrated its thousandth anniversary in 1975. Basically Romanesque in style, the dom is built of red sandstone, and has six impressive towers. Although dominating the square on which it is constructed, the huge building is tightly surrounded by houses, most of which date from the eighteenth century. The spacious interior contains many elaborate sculptures and monuments covering the wide period between the thirteenth and nineteenth centuries. The Cathedral Treasury and Museum (Dom und Diözesan Museum) contains many objects of fine art and ecclesiastical interest. The Saint Gothard Chapel dates from the twelfth century.

The spacious market square (Mainz Markt) in the central pedestrianised area was rebuilt after the Second World War. The Renaissance fountain here is called the Marktbrunnen.

The Haus zum Romischen Kaiser, on Liebfrauenplatz, houses the Gutenberg Museum, which details the life, times and work of the printer, and displays his most famous work, the Gutenberg Bible, one of the most important and beautiful printed books in the world. Gutenberg built the first machine to print from movable type in Mainz in 1456.

Although Mainz was severely bombed in World War Two, amazingly many fine old narrow streets containing several Renaissance and Gothic buildings have survived. Two of the old city gates still stand, the Eiserne Turm (Iron Tower) and the Holz Turm (Wooden Tower). The castle, a massive Renaissance/Baroque building, was the former palace of the Archbishop-Electors of Mainz. Today the palace houses the Römisch-Germanisches Museum (Royal German Museum). Other museums worth a visit are the large Landesmuseum, and Mainz Natural History Museum.

Two of the city's noteworthy churches are the Church of Saint Ignas (elaborate Rococco) and the fourteenth century Gothic Church of Saint Stephen. The latter, situated in Willigisplatz, contains several modern stained glass windows by Marc Chagall, based on the theme of reconciliation. The City Hall or *Rathaus* is modern, dating from the 1970s.

Those interested in European carnivals and festivals should note that Mainz has several, the most important being Johannisnacht in mid-June, Weinmarkt at the end of August and Nikolausfest in December.

SUMMARY

The countryside on the first part of today's route is similar to yesterday's, with vineyards and rolling hills continuing to dominate the landscape. The trail is still generally heading in an easterly direction. From the brows of these gentle hills there are good views of the Rhine valley. The trail visits the town of Heidesheim where one of the houses is a converted trullo (see above).

After Heidesheim the landscape changes again as the route enters the Mainzer woods, much frequented by strolling locals. Take care with navigation as there are many footpaths amongst the trees. The RHW passes the impressive Lenneberg Palace, before crossing over the A643 autobahn to enter the outer suburbs of Mainz. The last section of the walk, through the suburbs, can be omitted by taking public transport. Mainz itself, with its high cathedral dome and several interesting museums, is worth a day to itself.

THE ROUTE

At the Burgkirche in Ingelheim-Süd, walk to the right of the church,

The Burgkirche and restored old town walls, Ingelheim-Süd

pass through the stone archway and bear left behind the church to follow the surfaced lane through the vineyards, heading east-north-east: this is the Mainzer Weg.

The lane climbs quite steeply out of the valley, before levelling and continuing across a plateau. Remain on this surfaced track as it climbs again, now more gradually, to reach a spot-height of 228m, where there is a "dog-leg" in the lane. Seven hundred metres after this point turn left down a surfaced track, with trees to the left and an open field to the right. Three hundred metres later, at a T-junction, turn right along a grassy grit track. A hundred metres after crossing a lane the trail meets a main road. Cross this road to continue on the concrete track opposite. After almost a kilometre the track begins to descend towards the valley to the north. Where an expansive view of the Rhine valley ahead opens out, turn right on a track by a seat and a "Wasser-Schutzgebiet" signpost. After a while a wide view opens out to the left, of Heidesheim and the Rhine valley. Remain on the main track as it swings to the left at a seat and "Naturschutzgebiet" signpost. Keep to the main track as it descends to a second "Naturschutzgebiet" signpost at a track T-junction. Turn left here, downhill. Descend to reach a narrow, grassy footpath which starts immediately before a wooden telegraph pole ("R" waymark). Descend on this path through an orchard to emerge on a road in Heidesheim.

Bear left on this road (Ober-dorfstrasse), follow it round a left-hand bend and then turn right along Grabenstrasse. Bear right off this road within 100 metres, at a signpost for Pfingstborn, to walk alongside a high stone wall. Climb to a road and track junction, where turn left (north) with an orchard on the right and a field on the left. Descend on this track (An Der Bitz) to a track junction by houses; here turn right (east-south-east) for 100 metres and then left at the next track junction. Continue ahead to a track T-junction by a seat, where you bear right. The track climbs gradually to meet a surfaced lane by houses. Turn left here, downhill. Descend on this lane as it bends to the left and then to the right. After about 700 metres turn right off the lane onto a dirt track.

Climb on this sandy track, heading slightly north of east, and ignoring any side turnings, to reach a Y-junction, where you bear left. On reaching a café/restaurant continue ahead on a narrow footpath (horseriding prohibited sign) to reach a track T-junction: turn left here to take the underpass under the A60/E42 autobahn. Within 40 metres bear right onto a narrow footpath which runs parallel with the motorway for a while before pulling away from it to reach a surfaced lane at a hairpin bend. Bear left along this lane which soon passes a

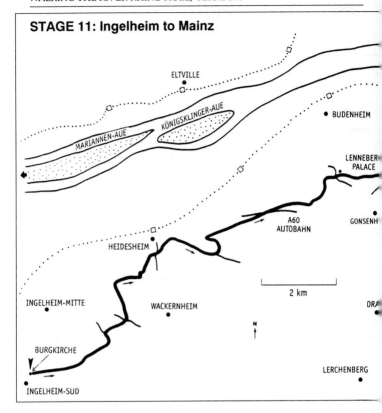

STAGE 11: Ingelheim to Mainz

hide/lookout tower on the left and continues through the woods. Take the right fork on reaching a Y-junction and continue ahead at the next cross-tracks, pass to the left of a spring and keep ahead, ignoring any side turnings. Just before reaching a road bear to the left on a forest track ("R" waymark). Bear left at the next junction, downhill. Turn right at a T-junction, to reach the Palace of Lenneberg.

Follow the drive of the palace eastwards to reach the gatehouse, and then a junction of main roads. Bear left, cross the main road (care) and take the minor road (bearing 40 degrees magnetic). After about 200 metres (stone tower ahead) turn right on a narrow footpath. After a further few hundred metres take a narrow "R" waymarked footpath

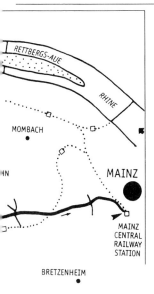

on the right. There is a maze of footpaths in these woods and the waymarking on the author's visit was not of a high standard. However, with perseverance, and following an easterly direction if in doubt, you should arrive at a large open-sided wooden shelter, situated in a clearing in the woods.

Follow the "R" waymarks eastwards from here, to reach a road. Turn right on the footpath in front of and parallel with this road, now heading south-east, to walk over the bridge over the A643 autobahn. Walk ahead to pass the attractive, brick-built Nothelferkapella. Bear left immed-iately after the church (*not* sharp left), following an "R" waymark. Keep to the surfaced path through this park, passing old stone "Stations of the Cross" and a small animal park (deer, wild boar, goats, etc.) to reach a road. Turn right (south-east) along this road and follow it for a kilometre along Kirchestrasse, heading towards the twin steeples of the church seen ahead.

Turn left at the T-junction immediately after the church to follow Mainzer Strasse. Keep ahead to cross Koblenzer Strasse (note that from here a bus can be taken to the centre of town). 1.4km after the church Mainzer Strasse crosses a railway line. Forty metres after this bear left along Am Fort Gonsenheim. After 1.3km this road reaches Wallstrasse. Cross the main road and bear right on the minor Fritz-Kohl-Strasse. Descend to the railway lines and bear right alongside them. Within a couple of hundred metres pass under the railway lines by means of an underpass, and then turn right along Kaiser-Wilhelm Ring to reach Mainz Haupt Bahnhof (main railway station). The tourist office (Verkehrs-Verein) and the railway station computer information system is opposite.

From the railway station walk ahead down Bahnhof Strasse, cross Grosse Bleiche, and follow the walkway sign to the dom (cathedral), along Schillerstrasse. Turn left onto Ludwigsstrasse to reach the mighty dom. Head east from the dom, past the Gutenberg Museum, to reach the Rhine.

145

STAGE 12
Mainz to Bodenheim: 13.8km (8.6 miles)

LOCATIONS	DISTANCES			
	Sectional		Accumulative	
	kms	miles	kms	miles
MAINZ (Town Centre)	-	-	229.2	142.3
Rhine (Theodar Heuss Brücke)	0.8	0.5	230.0	142.8
A60 (E42) Autobahn	5.9	3.7	235.9	146.5
BODENHEIM (100m; 329ft)	7.1	4.4	243.0	150.9

FACILITIES

The small town of Bodenheim, the end of this short section, has several small pensions (eg. Pension Königshof, Pension Angelica and Gästehaus "Zur Vroni"). It might be advisable to book ahead from Mainz Tourist Office.

For this section of the trail, and indeed for the last three days on the RHW to Alsheim, there is an option which deserves consideration. Instead of carrying all your gear and looking for accommodation in Bodenheim at the end of this day, and in Oppenheim at the end of tomorrow, and in Alsheim the night after that, you could simply book further nights in Mainz. There is such a frequent and fast train service between the towns en route that it would be perfectly feasible to walk each of the remaining stages whilst spending each overnight in Mainz. Today then, walk from Mainz to Bodenheim, returning by train to Mainz at the end of the walk. Take the train out to Bodenheim the following morning to continue the trail, returning to Mainz by train at the end of the day, this time from Oppenheim. The final stage between Oppenheim and Alsheim can be walked in exactly the same way. These tactics have two advantages: only a light sack need be carried, and there is no need to seek accommodation in Bodenheim, Oppenheim and Alsheim. Trains are frequent and relatively inexpensive. Mainz is a very pleasant city in which to have a base for a few days, with a wide choice of restaurants. Also, as the three stages from Mainz to the end of the trail at Alsheim are all rather short, you may decide to allow only two days for the walk to Alsheim. There are several other railway stations near the route that could be used to return to Mainz, eg. at Nackenheim and at Nierstein. Yet another option would be to take the train to Worms to find accommodation, from which city it would also be easy to return each day by rail to the RHW.

Today's stage between Mainz and Bodenheim is a relatively short one, and much of the first part is through the outskirts of Mainz, where refreshments are easily obtained. Bodenheim has a bakery, a delicatessen and several other small food shops. There is at least one restaurant in Bodenheim.

MAP
1:50,000: Mainz und Rheinhessen (Landesvermessungsamt Rheinland-Pfalz).

PLACES OF INTEREST

Mainz
See "Places of Interest" for Stage 11.

Wiesbaden
Wiesbaden is probably best seen on a day's visit whilst staying in Mainz. "Capital" of the Rheingau and the state capital of Hessen, it is situated on the right bank of the Rhine, almost opposite Mainz, at the confluence of the Rhine and the Main. Wiesbaden was founded over two thousand years ago by the Romans, who called the town Aquae Matticae, after the Mattici tribe. The attraction in Roman times, as in the nineteenth century when the city was in its heyday, was the thermal springs that abound in the area. One of the principal European spas, the aristocracy of the day came here in large numbers during the 1800s to "take the waters" (the famous healing waters can still be sampled today at the Kochbrunnen, not far from the Altes Rathaus in the centre of town). Today Wiesbaden remains up-market and expensive. The centre of town is dominated by the Kurhaus, built between 1890 and 1906, in which is housed the casino. Nearby is an elegant park, the Kurpark, and the main city theatre (Staatstheater). Wilhelmstrasse is at the heart of the expensive shopping area.

Buildings of interest to the visitor include the Altes Rathaus (Old Town Hall), the oldest building in Wiesbaden, the nineteenth century castle (Stadtschloss) and the Church of Saint Augustine of Canterbury. The name of this church indicates its original function when it was built in the nineteenth century to accommodate the many affluent

English visitors of the day.

Hochheim am Main
Hochheim is about 6km east of Mainz on the River Main, and can be easily reached by bus from either Mainz or Wiesbaden. The name "Hock" for the local white wine comes from here, the centre of a very famous wine growing area.

Bodenheim
Another wine village, Bodenheim has an attractive half-timbered *Rathaus* dating from 1608. The village also boasts a small museum (Heimatmuseum).

SUMMARY

Today's walk is a short, fairly easy one, so you should have plenty of time first to explore Mainz further, or to take transport for a half-day visit to Wiesbaden, or possibly even to Hochheim.

The Rhine, which has been heading eastwards since Bingen, makes another dramatic turn at Mainz towards the south. The rest of your journey, to the end of the Rheinhöhenweg at Alsheim, is now along paths and tracks heading to the south, through the region known as Rheinhessen. Woods are left behind after Mainz. You are now in open country, amidst vineyards and more gentle rolling hills. The walking from Mainz, for most of the way to Alsheim at the end of the trail, is along easy, mainly smooth tracks and paths - you may wish to walk in trainers if it is dry underfoot.

Several old, museum-type wine presses of historical interest are passed in the vineyards on the Rheinhöhenweg, particularly on these Mainz to Alsheim sections. Also several interpretive noticeboards are passed which provide information on the history and techniques of viticulture and wine making in the Rhine valley.

The three stages that constitute the remainder of the RHW are all fairly short in length, and are designed to provide a relaxing finale to the walk. You may wish to combine some of these stages. Most ramblers would find little difficulty in completing the route to Alsheim in two days as the walking is not arduous. Very fit and energetic walkers could even complete the route in one very long day. The choice is yours. The excellent transport along this final stretch allows for several possibilities (see "Facilities" above).

The first option, of course, is to omit the first stage of today's walk

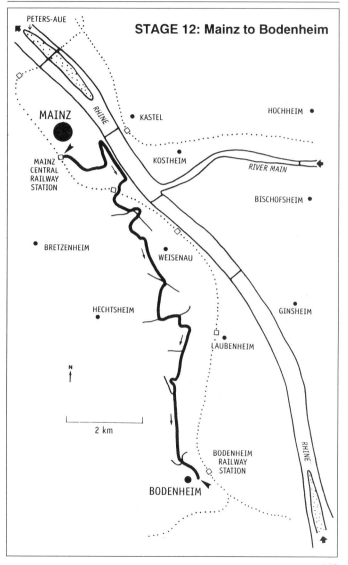

STAGE 12: Mainz to Bodenheim

PETERS-AUE

MAINZ

RHINE

KASTEL

HOCHHEIM

MAINZ CENTRAL RAILWAY STATION

KOSTHEIM

RIVER MAIN

BISCHOFSHEIM

BRETZENHEIM

WEISENAU

HECHTSHEIM

GINSHEIM

LAUBENHEIM

N

2 km

BODENHEIM RAILWAY STATION

RHINE

BODENHEIM

altogether by taking a bus to the outskirts of Mainz. However, the urban walk is quite pleasant and once the suburbs are behind you there is a terrace walk above the Rhine, all the way to the pretty wine village of Bodenheim, with first-rate views of the Rhine valley.

THE ROUTE

From the Theodor Heuss Brücke on the Rhine in the centre of Mainz, walk south-east along the left bank of the river for 1.2km, to the Winterhafen. Here turn right along Dagobertstrasse. At the main road continue ahead along Holzhofstrasse. At the end of this road bear slightly left to pass under a railway tunnel and ascend for 50 metres (high wall on left) to reach steps on the left. Climb these and then head south on the road signposted to the Krankenhäuser. At the traffic lights take the second turning on the left, bearing 120 degrees magnetic (*not* Auf Der Steig, which is first on the left, but Am Rosengarten - this name does not appear until later down this road). On reaching a junction with a main road turn left along An Der Favorite. Follow this road as it bends sharply to the right to reach a T-junction. Turn right to reach and cross Göttelmannstrasse. For the youth hostel turn left here.

To continue the Rheinhöhenweg cross the main road and follow the walkway ahead. After 400 metres emerge onto a road where you turn left, following the direction indicated by the signpost for the Theresianum. Where the road ends continue ahead on a dirt track. Turn left on reaching a T-junction and then right along Wilhelm-Th-Römheld-Strasse (fountain on right). Turn right at the T-junction ahead, but within 50 metres turn left along Heinrich-V. Brentano Strasse. Cross Weberstrasse and Jakob-Anstatt-Strasse to continue ahead on a surfaced "no through road". This leads to a footbridge over the A60 (E42) autobahn. Cross this and continue ahead, climbing to pass a metal cross dated 1985 and reach a T-junction by a small "Weisenau" memorial.

Turn left to follow the surfaced track to the left of a large field. Turn left on reaching a T-junction to walk along a road, but leave this for an earthen track on the right after about 200 metres. Keep to the left-hand edge of the field, remaining parallel with the road on your left to reach two finger posts. Turn right on a surfaced track at this point, signposted to Reiterverein Lothary-Aue. Turn left at a track junction at Gutshof-Laubenheimer-Höhe onto a dirt track to the right of vines. Within 300 metres turn right at a T-junction onto a surfaced track which heads south along the escarpment. Follow this track, above the town of Laubenheim, for 1.4km until, 150 metres after passing under HT electricity cables, a T-junction is reached. Turn right here and 100 metres later turn sharp left down an enclosed path. Bear right on reaching a track junction, and then within 25 metres, at a small stone building on the left, bear right again on another surfaced track with vines on the right and trees to the left. Now continue ahead, still heading south along the escarpment. Soon there is a "dog-leg" in the track, to right and left, after which you maintain direction, heading for Bodenheim, now clearly seen ahead. Descend towards the town. The track eventually swings to the left to reach the outskirts of Bodenheim. Keep ahead at a cross-tracks to enter the town. Bear right on reaching Schönbornplatz and walk along Obergasse, signposted to the Heimatmuseum.

STAGE 13
Bodenheim to Oppenheim: 16.9km (10.5 miles)

LOCATIONS	DISTANCES			
	Sectional		Accumulative	
	kms	miles	kms	miles
BODENHEIM (100m; 329ft)	-	-	243.0	150.9
Nackenheim	5.0	3.1	248.0	154.0
Nierstein	6.9	4.3	254.9	158.3
OPPENHEIM (100m; 329ft)	5.0	3.1	259.9	161.4

FACILITIES
Nierstein has several shops, cafés, restaurants and wine cellars.
Nackenheim has several shops. There is a hotel in Oppenheim, a bank
and a Wine Museum, as well as plenty of shops, cafés, bars and
restaurants. There is a campsite on the left bank of the Rhine, about
a mile east of Oppenheim railway station.

There are railway stations at Bodenheim, Nackenheim, Nierstein
and Oppenheim, all on the Mainz to Worms main line.

MAP
1:50,000: Mainz und Rheinhessen (Landesvermessungsamt
Rheinland-Pfalz).

PLACES OF INTEREST
Nackenheim
This wine village is famous as being the birthplace of the playwright
Carl Zuckmayer (1896-1979). Buildings of interest include the
eighteenth century *Rathaus* (Town Hall) and the Baroque Church of
Saint Gereon, the latter dating from 1716.

Nierstein
Another well-known wine town, with several attractive buildings,
and very many shops selling wine! Nierstein has two museums, both
of which are housed in the Altes Rathaus (Old Town Hall). These are
the Palaeontological Museum and the Schiffartmuseum (Shipping
Museum). The latter, which relates the history of shipping along the
Rhine, is rather interesting.

Nierstein has two notable churches. The Church of St Martin dates only from the eighteenth century, but has a twelfth century bell tower and an interesting fortified cemetery. The Baroque/ Romanesque Church of St Kilian is also eighteenth century. There is also a castle in the town. Perhaps the most interesting feature of Nierstein is the Stronabad, Roman Thermal Baths, discovered in 1802. These are on the outskirts of the town on the way to Oppenheim.

Oppenheim

Oppenheim, 5km south of Nierstein, is one of the most famous wine towns in Germany. It is an enchanting place, with many narrow, steep streets and attractive buildings. There is a pleasant market square surrounded by half-timbered houses. Oppenheim also has an interesting history, being known in Roman times as Bauconica, and later thought to have been the centre of Charlemagne's vast wine estates. Like many other towns in the region, Oppenheim was badly damaged by the French in 1688. The town originally lay directly on the banks of the Rhine itself, until the river was straightened in the nineteenth century. Oppenheim is said to be the warmest place in Germany!

Oppenheim's pièce de résistance is the Gothic Church of St Catherine (Katharinenkirche), not to be missed. Begun in 1226, the west towers and choir date from the thirteenth century, the nave is fourteenth century and the west end is fifteenth century, although the whole church was expertly restored between 1934 and 1937. The church contains a fourteenth century stained glass window called the Oppenheimer Rose. There is a small entrance charge. The church is open 8.00-18.00 in summer and 8.00-17.00 during the winter months. Not far from the Katharinenkirche is the Chapel and Charnel House of Saint Michael, which contains many human bones which are believed to date from the Thirty Years War.

There are several other places of interest in attractive Oppenheim, including the Gothic *Rathaus*, which dates from 1689, and the Deutsches Weinbaumuseum, which details the history and intricacies of wine production and viticulture. Finally, the fourteenth century Franciscan church of St Bartholomäus (Bartholomäuskirche) is also worth a look for its bizarre altar.

SUMMARY

There is little to write on this, the penultimate stage of the Rheinhöhenweg. If you enjoyed yesterday's stroll through the vineyards, you will surely love today's jaunt through similar countryside. There are a couple of good picnic spots on this stage, with picnic tables and benches. If you wish to plan ahead for your lunch stop then scan the route description below before starting your walk, as picnic spots are mentioned in the text. The first stage is a traverse of the vineyards to the small town of Nackenheim which has a very fine Baroque church. Then follows a superb Rhine Terrace walk, again through vineyards, with excellent views of the Rhine and the approaching town of Nierstein, which also has two fine churches, worth a quick look before continuing on to Oppenheim, at the end of today's stage. Oppenheim, which used to be the end point of the Rheinhöhenweg before it was extended to Alsheim, has what is surely the most impressive church of any German town of this small size. The stained glass of the Katharinenkirche is magnificent and a visit is highly recommended.

THE ROUTE

From the Heimatmuseum in Bodenheim continue along Obergasse. At the end of this road turn right onto Gaustrasse. Follow this road uphill to turn left onto Hellmerichstrasse. On approaching the church bear right along Lörzweiler Weg (signpost to Friedhof). The trail departs the town and heads south across the vineyards.

Cross a small stream and climb to a large wooden cross (picnic table). The Rheinhöhenweg is following the Kreuzweg over Kreuzberg. Continue on up the hill, walking ahead at a cross-tracks. At the next cross-tracks, a little before the crown of the hill, turn left ("R" waymark on stone to left of track). Continue to the point where the surfaced track ends. Here turn right on a grassy path for 100 metres to reach spot height 148m, where you turn left onto another grassy ride through the vines. Bear right with the track after 300 metres, and 150 metres later (small concrete construction on the right), turn left at a track junction, heading towards a pylon (onion dome of church half-right ahead). Bear right in front of the pylon. On reaching a solitary building (Marien-hof) bear right in front of it for 50 metres, and then follow the lane to the left to reach a road by another pylon. Turn left on the road to descend to the Baroque church

154

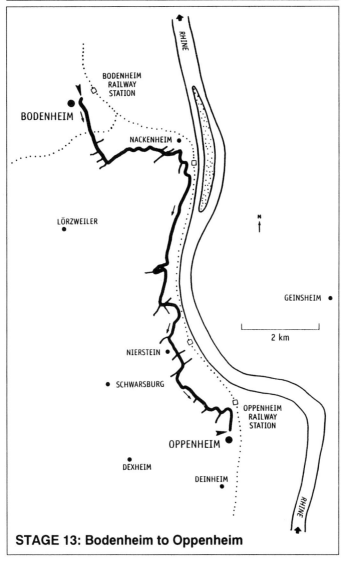

STAGE 13: Bodenheim to Oppenheim

at Nackenheim. Climb the steps on the left to visit this ornate building.

Turn right to head south on Langgasse and maintain direction at Carl-Zuckmayer-Platz, along Weinbergstrasse. After about 400 metres turn left up a narrow lane which begins by "Weingut Dr. Dietrich". Climb on this road, ignoring side turnings to the left, to pass "Marbé-Sans". Climb to a stone crucifix, on the right, where you turn left and continue to a T-junction by a seat, a large rock and a view over the Rhine. Turn right here to enjoy this Rhine Terrace Walk. On reaching a large cross on the left there is an exceptionally fine view of the Rhine and Nierstein.

Continue along the escarpment, passing a number of novel sculptures of vineyard workers. Eventually the trail negotiates a "dog-leg" to left and right. At this point be sure to take the lower of the two tracks to the right ("Spiegelberg" in large letters). This track descends for a short while before continuing as a terrace trail. A little over a kilometre later the trail passes an excellent picnic spot on the left, on a balcony overlooking the Rhine (there are five picnic tables and a dozen benches here, together with a large cross and flagpole).

Just after this picnic spot the trail bears away from the Rhine for 500 metres to the head of a small valley where it hairpins back to the left (do *not* be tempted to short-cut this detour by descending through the vines). Descend to take the next surfaced track on the right (no waymark here at the time of the author's visit). This track climbs a little around the hillside before resuming as a terrace track, passing the large letters "Hipping" on the hillside. Continue to a T-junction where you turn left, downhill. After about 200 metres turn right on a narrow paved path. This soon loses its paving to continue as a dirt track above vines. On reaching a T-junction at an old concrete fortification, turn left, downhill, to reach another track T-junction in front of the railway lines. Turn right here, passing beneath a Baroque church, to enter Nierstein at Kiliansweg.

Turn right on Breitgasse (south-west) to head towards the steeple of a second church. Bear left (south) at a T-junction to reach the centre of the town at Rheinstrasse. Bear right to walk along Oberdorfstrasse to the main town church. Continue to Uttrichstrasse, where you turn right, but 100 metres later turn left, now heading south-south-east. Walk ahead along this road (Bildstockstrasse), pass a football pitch on your right, continuing for 800 metres to reach a road T-junction at

A stone sculpture of a vinyard worker, sited amidst the vinyards above the Rhine, south of Nackenheim

Wörrstädter Strasse. Turn right for 200 metres to a minor road on the left. Ascend on this lane (Am Hummertal). Bear left on reaching a Y-junction by houses. Climb to a cross-tracks, where you turn left for 100 metres and then right on a concreted track through the vineyards. Turn left for 20 metres on meeting a T-junction and then right to maintain direction. On reaching a junction of two surfaced tracks and one unsurfaced track, turn left on the latter. After 250 metres turn right onto a stony track (large grassy area to the left). Turn left at a T-junction (steeples of Oppenheim church visible above the trees) onto Herrenbergweg, but where this swings sharply to the right after 100 metres, continue ahead on a dirt track to descend past the ruins of the large Releheburg Oppenheim, so leaving the Rhein Terrasse Wanderweg. Descend alongside the old castle walls to reach a road. Turn right to pass a stone tower and continue the descent alongside the castle walls and down into Oppenheim, passing immediately to the left of the large church (Katharinenkirche) to descend to the town centre.

STAGE 14
Oppenheim to Alsheim: 13.1km (8.1 miles)

LOCATIONS	DISTANCES			
	Sectional		Accumulative	
	kms	miles	kms	miles
OPPENHEIM (100m; 329ft)	-	-	259.9	161.4
Ludwigshöhe (near)	4.8	3.0	264.7	164.4
Guntersblum (near)	3.8	2.3	268.5	166.7
ALSHEIM 90m; 295ft)	4.5	2.8	273.0	169.5

FACILITIES
Accommodation is limited in Alsheim (although there is at least one *gasthaus*), so it might be advisable, on completion of the walk, to take a train back to Mainz or on to Worms. There is a small supermarket and a bakery in Alsheim. There are railway stations at Alsheim and Guntersblum.

Worms
Worms is approximately 16km (10 miles) by train, south of Alsheim. There is a wide choice of hotels and pensions in most price categories, as well as a youth hostel in Dechaneigasse, a street reasonably close to the cathedral. The tourist office is in the Neumarkt (No. 14). There is a campsite on the right bank of the Rhine near the Nibelungenbrüke (bridge over the Rhine). The main railway station (*Hauptbahnhof*) is northwest of the old city.

MAP
1:50,000: Mainz und Rheinhessen (Landesvermessungsamt Rheinland-Pfalz).

PLACES OF INTEREST
Guntersblum
There are principally two buildings of interest in the village, the Romanesque church and a Baroque building called the Adelshof, the latter originally belonging to the Teutonic Knights. A loop of the Rhine to the east of Guntersblum, created when the river was straightened in 1829, is the site of a nature reserve.

Street scene and the church at Oppenheim

Alsheim
Another attractive wine village, but of no particular interest save the fact that it is the terminus of the Rheinhöhenweg.

SUMMARY
So, after a fortnight's walking the final stage of the Rheinhöhenweg is now before you. Oppenheim to Alsheim, heading almost due south for the entire walk, offers another short stage, a pleasant gentle stroll through vineyards on a "Weinlehrpfad". There are fine and expansive views from this balcony path which passes, but never enters, a number of valley towns and villages: Dienheim, Ludwigshöhe and Guntersblum, before the RHW finally comes to an end in the small wine town of Alsheim. But take heart, there are still several opportunities for extending your holiday in the area (see "Epilogue" below). If time does not allow, however, say a final fond farewell to the Rhine by returning northwards along it on one of the Rhine cruises available from Mainz.

THE ROUTE
From the Katharinenkirche descend to Oppenheim town centre.

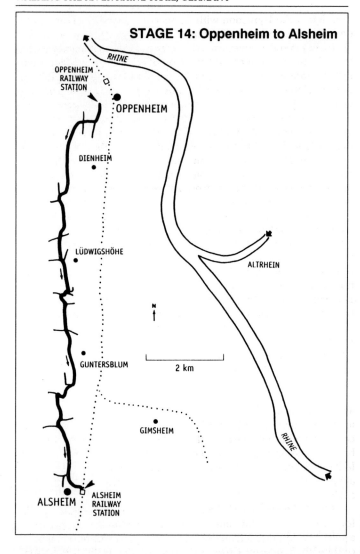

STAGE 14: Oppenheim to Alsheim

Turn left at the T-junction with Krämerstrasse and then turn right onto Wormser Strasse. Continue through the town, passing the Deutsches Weinbaumuseum. Where the road swings sharply to the left at Gartenstrasse, turn right (west) onto Sackträgerweg, signposted to Krötenbrunnen and the Weinlehrpfad. Continue ahead, uphill, on crossing the Weg Am Stadtgraben and again on crossing Güldenmorgenweg, and for a third time on crossing Kugelweg, but on reaching Reisekahrweg turn left to head southwards through the vineyards. Bear right, uphill, on reaching a Y-junction, remaining on Reisekahrweg, and ahead at the next junction at H Solweg. Bear left on reaching a T-junction ("R" and yellow "+" waymarks - the latter are those of the Saar-Rhein-Main Weg). Keep ahead, now climbing over Falkenberg, with the town of Dienheim below in the valley to the left. Take the left fork at the next Y-junction, onto a more minor track. This descends and then re-climbs to reach another track T-junction, where you bear left, maintaining a southerly direction.

After a further 300 metres the track turns to the right to head westwards to reach a T-junction. Turn left here. On reaching a small open stone building on the left, at a spot height of 181m, ignore the track immediately to its left and a footpath to the left 5 metres later, but turn on another track to the left, 5 metres after the footpath. This track turns at right angles to the right after 50 metres. Continue ahead now on this track, ignoring two side tracks on the left until after 700 metres our track bends to the right (west) to reach a T-junction. Turn left for 150 metres to meet a road. Bear slightly to the left, cross the road and continue ahead on a concreted track heading southwards and descending. The village of Ludwigshöhe is now down to your left. Ignore a track on the right and another on the left, but continue ahead to reach a T-junction (ignore track on right 20 metres before the junction). Turn left, downhill, for 80 metres to the point where the concrete track bends sharply to the left. Do not turn left with the track, but continue the descent ahead down a grassy bank (vines on your left) for a further 50 metres to meet another concrete track. Turn right along this ("R" and yellow cross waymarks) heading south once again.

After 800 metres the trail reaches a T-junction. Turn right, uphill, for 150 metres, left, downhill for 70 metres, and then right (west) to a junction. Now turn left downhill and left again at the next junction, continuing the descent. Cross a tiny stream (stone walled bridge) and

30 metres later ignore a track on the left. Remain on the track as it swings to right and to left, finally maintaining a southerly direction. Continue ahead at a cross-tracks, now descending on a paved path all the way to a road on the outskirts of Guntersblum. Turn right along this for 100 metres, before turning left at a Weinlehrpfad signpost. Bear right in front of the Reblausstube, and left (Weinlehrpfad sign) at the next junction. Follow the track downhill to turn right at a T-junction (seat and view of Guntersblum).

Continue ahead, later ignoring a track on the left down to Guntersblum and then passing above the town's two soccer pitches. On reaching a drainage ditch and solitary boulder on the left, turn right, uphill, for 80 metres and then left at a cross-tracks, now leaving Guntersblum behind. Remain on this surfaced track as it swings towards the west to reach a small stone bridge above a drainage ditch, at a cross-tracks. Turn left, south, here. Continue to reach buildings at Hangen-Wahlheim. Pass to the right of Oalberger-Hof and bear left at the junction beyond. The trail soon starts a descent and becomes a sunken track. Remain on this track as it heads towards Alsheim. The trail eventually reaches Wahlheimer Weg on the outskirts of Alsheim. Turn left on meeting the main road, so heading into the village. At the junction between Kesselgasse and Mittelgasse bear right onto the latter. Bear left at the next junction with Taubertstrasse to reach Bachstrasse. Turn left along this principal village street to reach the church. Turn right behind the church onto Gimbsheimer Strasse and then right along Raiffeisenstrasse to reach Alsheim Railway Station, Journey's End.

EPILOGUE

The trail terminates at Alsheim. Apart from leaving for home without further delay, there are a number of options you may be able to consider. You may like to return to Bonn on foot by following the Right Bank Trail of the Rheinhöhenweg. Or you may like to experience a boat cruise along the Rhine, or visit some of the other interesting towns and cities in the vicinity. Indeed it would be a pity to leave this most attractive area of Germany without at least visiting Worms and/or Frankfurt and/or Mannheim. Notes on these various options follow.

Rheinhöhenweg - Right Bank Trail

Those wishing to return to Bonn by walking the right or northern bank of the Rhine will first have to take a train back to Mainz and on to Wiesbaden where the Right Bank Trail of the Rheinhöhenweg begins.

Those with a reading knowledge of German would be able to use the guide booklet entitled simply *Rheinhöhenweg*, published by Rheinland-Pfalz, and available, usually free of charge, by sending an International Reply Coupon to Fremdenverkehrs und Heilbäderverband Rheinland-Pfalz (see Appendix D). This contains brief details of both the Left Bank RHW (the subject of this guidebook) and the Right Bank RHW. Alternatively, by using the maps, which have the route of both the Left Bank and the Right Bank clearly overlaid, you should have few problems of navigation, as the Right Bank Trail is also clearly waymarked on the ground with "R" (for "Rheinhöhenweg") waymarks.

The same maps at 1:50,000 scale are required for the Right Bank Trail as for the Left Bank Trail (see "Maps" in the Introduction for details), with the addition of the sheet entitled "Naturpark Rhein-Taunus", published by Hessisches Landesvermessungsamt (this sheet is for the southern end of the Right Bank Trail around and to the west of Wiesbaden). Note also that the "Mainz und Rheinhessen" 1:50,000 sheet necessary for the Left Bank Trail is not required for the Right Bank Trail.

If you do not have a guide to the Right Bank Trail the following information may be useful:

RHEINHÖHENWEG - RIGHT BANK TRAIL
Wiesbaden to Bonn-Beuel
Distance: 272km (169 miles)

The outline of the trail is as follows:

Wiesbaden > Schlangenbad > Stephanshausen > Aulhausen > Rüdesheim > Lorch > Sauertal > Kaub > Burg Gutenfels > Blüchertal > Dörscheid > Rossstein > Alten Burg > Urbachtal > Bornich > Waldschule > Lennigwald > Bornichbach > Aussiedlerhof Leiselfeld > Loreley-Felsen > Ortsteil Heide > Burg Katz > St Goarshausen > Burg Maus > Prath > Lykershausen > Bornhofen > Kamp > Osterspai > Braubach > Oberlahnsteiner Wald > Oberlahnstein > Niederlahnstein > Lichterkopf > Ehrenbreitstein > Kaiser-Friedrich-Turm > Meisenhof > Sayn > Friedrichberg > Oberbieber > Rengsdorf > Altwied > Monrepos > Christianshütte > Moselborn / Jakobshof > Leutesdorf > Forsthof > Annahof > Rheinbrohl > Bad Hönningen > Ariendorf > Leubsdorf > Dattenberg > Linz > Erpeler Ley > Unkel > Bad Honnef > Margarethenhöhe > Einkehrhaus > Dollendorfer Haardthütte > Beuel.

Beuel is a suburb of Bonn, on the right bank of the river, opposite Bonn city. The trail terminates at Beuel Railway Station.

The trail, like that on the left bank, is a "high level" one, frequently undulating. It often keeps well away from the river, preferring the delectable countryside to the north, and so bypasses several of the main resorts and towns on the right bank of the Rhine. However, many of these can easily be visited by waymarked spur routes from the main trail.

As with the Left Bank Trail there is adequate accommodation of all types in the many villages, towns and cities passed en route. If in doubt contact the tourist offices in the area.

Boat Cruise or Scenic Train Journey along the Rhine

Either take the famous scenic train that runs the length of the river back to Bonn or Cologne, or, even better, board one of the many cruise boats that ply the river. KD-Lines are the main carriers. Although rather expensive, and often full with tourists, the boat journey along this most famous and scenically attractive of European rivers will remain a pleasant memory. Indeed, perhaps the best way of seeing and enjoying the Rhine and its numerous attractive villages, towns, castles, gorges and surrounding hills is from the water itself. The most scenic section of the river is between Bingen and Koblenz. I would recommend taking a River Rhine cruise from Mainz, downriver to Koblenz, a journey of about $5^1/_2$-6 hours (slow Rhine Cruise boats), and from there finally make your way home by plane or train.

Worms

Worms is16km (10 miles) south of the trail end at Alsheim, and is easily reached from there by train (frequent, daily services).

Settlements in the Rhineland often have long histories, many going back to Roman times. But the city of Worms goes back even further, being one of the oldest German cities, with over 6000 years of history. The original Celtic settlement on this site was called Borbetomagus, whereas to the later Romans it was Civitas Vangionum. The former Imperial city is of significant historical importance, one of the principal centres of the Holy Roman Empire. It was at Worms in 1122 that a Concordat was signed which settled the conflicts between Pope and Emperor. Charlemagne and Barbarossa were both married at Worms. During medieval times there were many important Diets or Imperial Parliaments there, notably that of 1521, when Martin Luther was called to justify his revolutionary religious ideas, the result of which led to the greatest schism that the Christian Church has ever witnessed, with the formation of the Protestant faith (seek out Lutherdenkmal where there are nineteenth century statues of Luther and other notables of the Protestant Reformation). Like many of its neighbouring towns and cities Worms has been destroyed several times throughout its long history, the most notable sacking being that by a Swedish army during the Thirty Years War.

In legend the city is also of great importance, as it lies at the heart of the Nibelungen epic, the greatest of the German legends, which centres on a Burgundian tribe which lived here during the fifth century, and whose story is related in the *Nibelungenlied*, the great saga written at the end of the twelfth century.

Worms is the home of the most well known of all German wines: Liefraumilch. The vineyard originally associated with this wine is adjacent to the Liebfrauenkirche, although, not surprisingly, vineyards entirely surround the city.

The main attraction to visitors is the Romanesque Cathedral of St Peter, built during the eleventh and twelfth centuries on the site of an earlier Roman forum. The building consists of four large, round towers and an octagonal cupola and inside has an elaborate Baroque High Altar and several Romanesque and Gothic statues. There are several other churches of note in the city including the eleventh century Collegiate Church of St Andrew, the ninth century Church of St Magnus, and the Church of Our Lady and Church of the Holy Trinity (Dreifaltigkeit Church), the latter a simple Lutherian Church.

Worms was one of most important Jewish cities in Europe, large communities of Jews thriving here from the tenth century until the Nazi era. The synagogue, founded in the eleventh century, was the oldest in Germany, but was destroyed in 1938, although rebuilt in 1961. The Jewish Cemetery, the oldest and largest in Europe, is located in the Judenfriedhof. The history of the Jews in Worms is told in the Judaica Museum, and the city has several buildings and monuments erected by the Jewish community.

The major city museum is the Städtisches Museum (Municipal Museum). Tourist Information Office at Neumarkt 14.

Frankfurt

As Frankfurt am Main is the site of Germany's main international airport, you may wish to set aside a day to explore this city before leaving. A modern city of many skyscrapers and other futuristic buildings, it is the commercial heart of Germany, Frankfurt has much to offer the discerning visitor. There are very many museums, art galleries, churches and notable buildings that would easily occupy a day or more. Any tour of the city should try to cover the principal highlights which include the Hauptwache, Römerberg Square, the Altstadt, Cathedral, the Goethehaus and Goethemuseum, Sachsenhausen and the Städelsches Kunstinstitut & Städtische Galerie (Art Institute and Municipal Gallery - this houses one of the most important art collections in Germany). The main tourist office is at Römerberg 27 (tel. [069] 212 38708), but there is also an information centre at the main railway station (*Hauptbahnhof*) and another at the airport.

Mannheim

The city of Mannheim, to the south of the area covered by this guidebook, is also worth a visit. Situated at the confluence of the Rivers Rhine and Neckar, it is an important river port, the second largest in Europe. Although industrial in nature, it is an attractive, elegant town, based on a chessboard grid layout of streets, unusual for Europe, which dates from the seventeenth century. The main attractions for the visitor are the massive Baroque Electoral Palace, which now houses the university, the Jesuit Church (Jesuitenkirche), the largest and one of the most important Baroque churches in Germany, and the Städtische Kunsthalle (City Art Museum). There are tourist offices at the main railway station and at the airport.

APPENDIXES

A: YOUTH HOSTELS ON OR NEAR THE RIVER RHINE TRAIL

A German Youth Hostel is usually abbreviated to DJH (Deutsche Jugendherberge). The hostels below are listed from north to south, as they would be encountered when walking the trail from Bonn to Alsheim. When making an enquiry or sending a booking, address your letter as follows: The Jugendherberge (DJH), Postcode, Name of Town, Germany. Do not use British second class post (not valid for the EU) and always enclose an International Reply Coupon, available from most British Post Offices. For a full, up-to-date list of German Youth Hostels write to the German Youth Hostels Association (see Appendix D).

In the following list the name of the village/town/city in which the hostel is situated is given, followed by the postcode. Their actual locations are shown on the recommended 1:50,000 maps. Note that Bonn and Köln (Cologne) both have two youth hostels.

Bonn - Venusberg, JGH
Haager Weg 42, D-5300

Bonn - Bad Godesberg, JGH
Horionstrasse 60, D-5300

Bad Honnef
Selhofer Strasse 106, D-5340
(off-route, on the right bank of the Rhine)

Bad Neuenahr-Ahrweiler, JGH
D-5483 (a considerable distance off-route, in the Ahr valley)

Koblenz
Festung Ehrenbreitstein
Ehrenbreitstein, D-5400
(on the right bank of the Rhine, opposite Deutsches Eck)

St Goar
Bismarckweg 17, D-5401

St Goarshausen
Auf Der Loreley, D-5422
(on the right bank of the Rhine, not far from the Lorelei rocks)

Oberwesel, JGH, D-6532
(passed en route of the RHW, on leaving Oberwesel, heading south)

Bacharach
Jugendburg Stahleck
Schlossberg, D-6533

Bingen-Bingerbrück
Herter Strasse 51, D-6530
(in the suburb of Bingerbrück)

Rüdesheim
Am Kreuzberg, D-6220
(on the right bank of the Rhine, opposite Bingen)

Mainz, JGH
Am Fort Weisenau, D-6500

Wiesbaden
Blücherstrasse 66, D-6200
(on the right bank of the Rhine, opposite Mainz)

Other youth hostels that may be of use when travelling to and from the region are listed below.
At the northern end of the trail:
(Cologne) Köln
Siegesstrasse, Deutz 21, D-5000
(Cologne) Köln
An der Schanz 14, Riehl 60, D-5000

Düsseldorf JH 80, JGH 200

Düsseldorfer Strasse 1, D-4000

Mönchengladbach/Hardter Wald
D-4050

At the southern end of the Trail:
Worms

Dechaneigasse 1, D-6520
(not far from the Cathedral)

Frankfurt am Main 70
Deutschherrnufer 12, D-6000

Mannheim
Rheinpromenade 21, D-6800

B: USEFUL GERMAN WORDS AND PHRASES

Emphasis has been placed on words likely to be of use to walkers and travellers in Germany, seeking direction, assistance, accommodation, food and refreshment. Remember that all syllables are pronounced in German.

GERMAN	ENGLISH	GERMAN	ENGLISH
Abend	Evening	Brunnen	Fountain or Well
Abendessen	Dinner or Supper	Brücke	Bridge
Abfahrt	Departure	Burg	Castle or Fortress
Allee	Lane, Alley	Büro	Office
Altstadt	Old part of a town or city	Bäckerie	Baker's
		Damen (as a sign)	Women's Toilets
Ampel	Traffic Lights	Danke/Danke Schön	Thank You/Thank you very much
Ankunft	Arrival		
Apfel	Apple	DB (Deutsche Bahn)	German National State Railways
Apotheke	Chemist's, Pharmacy		
Arzt	Doctor	Dienstag	Tuesday
Auf Wiedersehen	Goodbye	Dom	Cathedral
Ausgang	Exit	Donnerstag	Thursday
Aussichtspunkt	Viewpoint	Dorf	Village
Autobahn	Motorway	Dusche	Shower
Bach	Stream	Ecke	Corner
Bad	Bath	Ei	Egg
Bahnhof	Railway Station	Ein/zwei/drei	One/two/three
Bahnsteig	Railway Platform	Einbahnstrasse	One way street
Bank	Seat or Bench	Eingang	Entrance
Bauernhaus	Farmhouse	Einzäunung	Fence or hedge
Baum	Tree	Eis	Ice-cream
Berg	Mountain or Hill	Eisenbahn	Railway
Besucherzentrum	Visitors' Centre	Entschuldigen Sie	Excuse me
Bier	Beer	Erdbeere	Strawberry
Billig	Cheap	Essen	Food
Birne	Pear	Fahrkarte	Ticket (to Travel)
Bitte/Bitte schön	Please	Fahrplan	Timetable
blau	blue	Feiertag	Bank Holiday
Blick or Anblick	View or Viewpoint	Festung	Fortress
braten	roast	Fisch	Fish
Brot	Bread	Fleisch	Meat

GERMAN	ENGLISH	GERMAN	ENGLISH
Flughafen	Airport	Heiss	Hot
Fluss	River	Herren (as a sign)	Men's Toilets
Forelle	Trout	Heute	Today
Frauen (as a sign)	Women's Toilets	Holzspanweg	Path surfaced with
Frei platz	Vacant seat (on a		wood chippings
	train, etc)	Huhn	Chicken
Freitag	Friday	Hügel	Hill
Frucht	Fruit	Ich verstehe nicht	I don't understand
Frühstück	Breakfast	Imbiss (Imbiss Stube)	Snack Bar
Fussgänger	Pedestrian	Jahr	Year
Fussgängerbrücke	Footbridge	Jugendherberge (DJH)	Youth Hostel
Fussgängerunter-	Pedestrian Safety	Kaffee	Coffee
führung	Barrier	Kalbfleish	Veal
Fussgängerübergang	Pedestrian Crossing	kalt	cold
Fussweg	Footpath	Kanal	Canal
Grüss Gott	Greeting (mainly in	Kapelle	Chapel
	southern Germany)	Karte	Map
Guten Abend	Good Evening	Kartoffel	Potato
Guten Morgen	Good Morning	Kein Eingang	No Entrance
Guten Tag	Good Day	Kiesweg	Gravel Track
Gabelung	Junction	Kino	Cinema
Gasse	Alley	Kirche	Church
Gasthaus	Guest House	kleine	small
Gasthof	Guest House	Klinkerweg	Cobbled track, road
gegenüber	opposite		or path
gekocht	boiled	Kloster	Monastery or
gelp	yellow		Convent
Gemüse	Vegetables	Kohl	Cabbage
Geöffnet	Open (of a shop, etc)	Konditorei	Cake Shop
Gepäck	Luggage	Kotelett	Chop
geradeaus	straight on	Krankenhaus	Hospital
Geschlossen	Closed (of a shop,etc)	Kreuzung	Junction, Cross-
Gestern	Yesterday		tracks, Crossroads
Gipfel	Peak, summit	Kreuzweg	Junction, Cross-
Gleis	Railway Track		tracks, Crossroads
Graben	Ditch	Kuchen	Cake
Gras	Grass	Kurve	Bend
gross	large	Käse	Cheese
grün	green	Lamm	Lamb
Hauptbahnhof	Principal Railway	Landweg	Track (unmetalled)
Station		Männer (as a sign)	Men's Toilets
Hauptstrasse	High Street	Markt	Market
Haus	House	Marmelade	Jam
Heide	Heather moorland	Milch	Milk
	or heath	Mittagessen	Lunch

GERMAN	ENGLISH	GERMAN	ENGLISH
Mittwoch	Wednesday	Schokolade	Chocolate
Monat	Month	Schranke	Barrier
Montag	Monday	schwarz	black
Morgen	Morning (used as a greeting)	Schweinefleisch	Pork
		See	Lake
Morgen	Tomorrow	Sonnabend	Saturday (only in North Germany)
Morgen früh	Tomorrow morning		
Münster	Minster	Sonntag	Sunday
nach links	turn left	Speck	Bacon
nach oben	uphill	Stadt	Town or City
nach rechts	turn right	Steg	Small Bridge
Nachspeise	Dessert	Strasse	Street
nach unten	downhill	Strassenbahn	Tram
Nacht	Night	Stufe	Stile
Naturlandschaft	Nature Reserve (protected)	Supermarkt	Supermarket
		Suppe	Soup
Naturpark	Nature Park (protected)	Tag	Day
		Tal	Valley
Nicht rauchen	No smoking	Tankstelle	Petrol Station
Notausgang	Emergency Exit	Tee	Tea
Obst	Fruit	TEE	Trans European Express train
Parkplatz	Car Park		
Pass	Passport	Teuer	Expensive
Pfad	Path	Theater	Theatre
Pfahl	Markerpost	Toilette	Toilet
Plattenweg	Paved footpath	Tor	Gate or Gateway
Platz	Square (in village, town or city)	Torte	Gateau
		Treppe	Flight of Steps or Stairs
Polizei	Police or Police Station		
		Turm	Tower or Spire
Postamt (Post)	Post Office	Umleitung	Diversion
Radweg	Cycle Path	Verboten	Forbidden; Prohibited
Rathaus	Town Hall		
Reis	Rice	Verkehrsamt	Tourist Office
Reisebüro	Travel Agent	Verkehrsverein	Tourist Office
Reitweg	Bridleway	Verkehrsweg	Main Road (usually busy with motor traffic)
Richtung	Direction		
Rindfleisch	Beef	Vielen Dank	Thank you very much
rot	red	Vorsicht!	Attention
Ruhetag	Closed or Rest Day	Vorspeise	Hors d'oeuvre
Sahne	Cream	Wald	Wood or Forest
Samstag	Saturday	wander	to walk, ramble, hike
Schild	Signpost	Wanderer	Walker, Rambler,
Schinken	Ham		
Schloss	Castle or Palace		

170

GERMAN	ENGLISH	GERMAN	ENGLISH
	Backpacker	Woche	Week
Wanderkarte	Map specifically intended for walkers	Wochenende	Weekend
		Wo ist....	Where is....
Wanderstrecke	Walking route or trail	Wurst	Sausage
Wanderweg	Walking trail	Zahnarzt	Dentist
Wasser	Water	Zaun	Gate or Fence
Weg	Path, Route, Way, Road, Trail	Zimmer	Room
		Zimmer frei	Rooms available
Weide	Field	Zitrone	Lemon
Wein (rot, weiss)	Wine (red, white)	Zoll	Customs
weiss	white	Zucker	Sugar
weiterlaufen	go straight on	Zug	Train
Wechsel	Money Exchange	Zutritt frei	Entry allowed; free access
Werth	An island in the Rhine		
Wiedersehen	Goodbye	Zutritt verboten	No Entry
Wies	Field or Meadow		

C: BIBLIOGRAPHY

1. *A Time of Gifts* by Patrick Leigh Fermor (1977). Penguin Travel Library. The story of a walk from Rotterdam to Hungary, much of it through prewar Germany, undertaken in 1933/34 when the author was an adolescent, the account of his journey written in a superb prose style some 40 years later. A significant part of his journey followed the Rhine. An enlightened insight into a Germany in the grip of Nazi fascism. Winner of the 1978 W.H. Smith Literary Award.

2. *The Rhine. An Insight Guide* (First Edition, 1991). APA Publications (HK). Written by a number of specialist authors, this guidebook includes practical information and a considerable section on the history and culture of the area surrounding the great river. Look out for the latest edition.

3. *To the End of the Rhine* by Bernard Levin (1987). Jonathan Cape. The book of the Channel Four series charting the journey of the well known journalist from near the source of the river in the Swiss Alps to the Rhine Delta at the North Sea in Holland.

4. *The Nibelungenlied* Translated by A.H. Hatto. Penguin Classics. The story of this epic German poem, written around AD 1200, formed the basis of Richard Wagner's momentous music drama *Der Ring des Nibelungen*. This is a very readable translation. Much of the story centres on the Rhine and its environs.

5. *Legends of the Rhine* by Wilhelm Ruhland. Out of print, but worth looking for in second-hand bookshops or library. Detailed accounts of the principal myths and legends associated with the great European river.

6. General Guidebook to Germany: *Germany - The Rough Guide*. Includes useful information on the Rhineland. Be sure to purchase the latest edition.

7. General Guidebook to Germany: *Blue Guide to Western Germany* by James Bentley. A & C Black. An alternative purchase to *The Rough Guide* above, which like the latter, is primarily intended for independent travellers, but which has rather more emphasis on history, art and architecture. The book includes a chapter on the Rhine valley. Likewise be sure to purchase the latest edition.

8. *Exploring Rural Germany* by John Ardagh (1990). Christopher Helm. This book contains a concise and informative chapter on the Rhineland.

9. *Visitor's Guide to Germany: Rhine & Mosel* by John Marshall (1992). Moorland Publishing.

10. *On Foot Through Europe: A Trail Guide to West Germany* by Craig Evans (1982). Quill. Out-of-print and a lot of the detailed information is now very much out-of-date. Nevertheless it is still worth chasing up a copy of this book, written as part of a European series of "Trail Guides" by the former Director of the American Hiking Society and former Editor of the American Backpacker Magazine. It still contains more information in English on walking in Germany than any other publication, to this author's knowledge.

11. *Europäischer Fernwanderweg E 8* by Gert Trego. In German. Concise guidebook to the E 8 Long Distance Footpath, over 2000km from Amsterdam, through Holland, Germany and north-eastern Austria to Bratislava. About 60 percent of the route is through Germany and is coincident with the Rheinhöhenweg for much of the way between Bonn and Bacharach/Bingen. No sketch maps are included. The author, an Austrian, is well known in German speaking countries as a European long distance walker.

12. *European Long Distance Footpaths (Europäische Fernwanderwege/Sentiers Européens de Grande Randonnée).* Booklet published in English, German and French by the European Ramblers' Association (see "Useful Addresses"). Brief details of the eleven long distance E trails which cover most European countries and have a total length of over 35,000kms. The majority of the E routes pass through Germany, which, of course, has a central position in Europe. Include an International Reply Coupon with your request for this free publication.

13. *Thomas Cook European Timetable.* Railway and Shipping Services throughout Europe. Published monthly. Includes the principal train services operated by Deutsche Bahn (DB), the German National Railway Company.

14. *Michelin Deutschland.* Published annually. Contains comprehensive listings of hotels and restaurants in Germany, including those in the towns and cities visited on the River Rhine Trail.

D: USEFUL ADDRESSES

Note that addresses and telephone numbers of organisations sometimes change with time.

General information:

1. German National Tourist Office. 65 Curson Street, London W1Y 7PE. Tel (0891) 600100 (Information Line).

2. Regional Addresses. Write or telephone for general tourist information on the area:

    i)   Fremdenverkehrs und Heilbäderverband Rheinland-Pfalz e.V. Löhrstrasse 103-105, D-56068, Koblenz (or Postfach 1420, D-56014 Koblenz), Germany. Tel (+49) (0261) 31079. Fax (+49) (0261) 18343.

    ii) Landesverband Rheinland e.V. Düsseldorfer Strasse 1, D-4000, Düsseldorf 11, Germany. Tel (+49) (0211) 577030. Fax (+49) (0211) 579735.

    iii) Nordrhein-Westfalen. Landesverkehrsverband Rheinland, Postfach 200861, D-5300, Bonn 2, Germany. Tel (+49) (0228) 36 29 21 or (+49) (0228) 36 29 22.

    iv) Landesverband Rheinland-Pfalz/Saarland e.V. In der Meielache 1, D-6500, Mainz, Germany. Tel (+49) (06131) 320095. Fax (+49) (06131) 31325.

    v)   FVV Rheinland-Pfalz, Postfach 1420, D-5400, Koblenz, Germany. Tel (+49) (0261) 31079.

3. German National Travel Agency. DER. 18 Conduit Street, London W1R 9TD.

Maps and guidebooks:

4. Edward Stanford Ltd. 12-14 Long Acre, London WC2E 9LP. Tel (0171) 836 1321.

5. Latitude Maps & Globes. 34 The Broadway, Drakes Lane, Potters Bar, Herts EN6 2HW. Tel (01707) 663090.

6. Maps by Mail. P.O. Box 350A, Surbiton, Surrey KT5 9LX. Tel (0181) 399 4970.

7. The Map Shop. 15 High Street, Upton-upon-Severn, Worcestershire WR8 0HJ.

Any of these specialist map shops should either have German maps in stock or will be able to order them on your behalf. Alternatively, contact direct the relevant regional German Map companies given below for map catalogues, etc:

8. LVA Nordrhein-Westfalen. Muffendorfer Strasse 19-21, Postfach 205007, D-53170, Bonn 2, Germany. Tel (+49) (0228) 846535.

9. LVA Rheinland-Pfalz. Postfach 1428, D-56014, Koblenz, Germany. Tel (+49) (0261) 492232, Fax (+49) (0261) 492492.

10. Hessisches Landesvermessungsamt. Postfach 3249, D-65022 Wiesbaden, Germany. Tel (+49) (0611) 535236.

Walking organisations:
11. European Ramblers' Association (ERA). Europäische Wandervereinigung e.V. Reichsstrasse 4, Postfach 10 32 13, D-66032, Saarbrücken, Germany. Tel. (+49) (0681) 390070. Fax 49-681 3904650. Details of the European International Long Distance Footpaths (E routes) and general information on walking in Germany and Europe.
12. Verband Deutscher Gebirgs und Wandererverine, Postfach 401, D-6800 Saarbrücken, Germany. Walking and mountaineering organisation.
13. Local Walking Organisations:
    i)   Verein Linker Niederrhein. Karlsplatz 14, D-4150, Krefeld 1, Germany.
    ii) Eifelverein. Postfach 646, D-5160, Düren, Germany.
    iii) Hunsrückverein. D-6561, Kempfeld/Wildenburg, Germany.
    iv) Pfälzerwald-Verein. Fröbelstrasse 26, D-6730 Neustadt/Weinstrasse, Germany.

Hostel type accommodation:
14. German Youth Hostel Association (DJH):
    Deutsches Jugendherbergswerk. Hauptverband für Jugendwandern und Jugendherbergen e. V., Bismarckstrasse 8 (Postfach 220), D-4930 Detmold, Germany. Tel (+49) (05231) 74010. Fax (+49) (05231) 7401 49. Contact the Association for a full and up-to-date list of youth hostels in Germany.
15. Naturfreunde:
    Touristenverein die Naturfreude, Postfach 380, D-7000, Stuttgart 60, Germany. Tel (+49) (0711) 337687 or (+49) (0711) 337688. Send for details of their hostels (Naturfreundehäuser).

Airline operators to Germany:
16. Lufthansa (German National Airlines). 10 Old Bond Street, London W1X 4EN. Tel (0345) 737 747.
17. British Airways. 156 Regent Street, London W1R 5TA. Tel (0181) 759 8181 (Helpline), (0181) 759 2525 (Flight Information), (0345) 222111 (Reservations).
18. KLM-UK. Stansted House, Stansted Airport, Essex CM24 1AE. Tel (0990) 074074. Flights to Frankfurt and Düsseldorf.
19. DebonAir. Tel (0500) 146200. Flights to Mönchengladbach.

Rail services to Europe:
20. British Rail European Enquiries. Tel (0171) 834 2345.

Coach services to Europe:
21. National Express Coach Services. Eurolines. Victoria Coach Station, London SW1. Tel (0171) 730 0202 or (0171) 730 8235. Details of coach services between the UK and Germany.

Channel Tunnel services:
22.   Eurostar. Waterloo International Terminal, London SE1 7LT. Tel (0345) 881881. Direct train services to Europe via the Channel Tunnel.
23.   Le Shuttle (car transporter through the Channel Tunnel).
       Le Shuttle Call Centre, tel (0990) 35 35 35.
       Le Shuttle Agentline, tel (0990) 51 52 53.

Cross Channel Ferry/Hovercraft operators:
24.   P & O European Ferries. Channel House, Channel View Road, Dover CT17 9TJ. Tel (01304) 203388, or (0181) 575 8555, or (0990 980 980).
25.   Sealink Stena Line. Charter House, PO Box 121, Park Street, Ashford, Kent TN24 8EX. Tel (01233) 647047 or (0990)70 70 70
26.   North Sea Ferries. King George Dock, Hedon Road, Hull, N. Humberside HU9 5QA. Tel (01482) 77177.
27.   Sally Line Ferries. Sally Line Ltd, 81 Piccadilly, London W1V 9HF. Tel (0171) 409 2240 or at Ramsgate, Tel (01843) 595522.
28.   Hoverspeed: Maybrook House, Queen's Gardens, Dover CT17 9UQ. Tel (01304) 240101.

Travel insurance:
29.   Thomas Cook Group Ltd. PO Box 36. Thorpe Wood, Peterborough PE3 6SB. Tel (01733) 63200. Ask for details of their Independent Travellers Insurance Scheme.

※　※　※